Seeking
Surrender

"Colette Lafia challenges our notion of surrender, inviting us to see it as a path of opening to the fullness of life. Her spiritual companion, a Trappist monk from the Abbey of Gethsemani, encourages and guides her toward deeper trust along her journey in a series of letters shared over years. A beautiful and honest book."

Richard Rohr, O.F.M.
Center for Action and Contemplation

"Surrender to the will of God is discovered as foundational in this intriguing spiritual journey based on a seven-year correspondence between Colette Lafia and a simple Trappist brother who was overcome with his love for God. *Seeking Surrender* is a rewarding read for those searching for an answer in the midst of darkness only to discover he is always with us."

Damien Thompson, O.C.S.O.
Former Abbot
Abbey of Gethsemani

"Weaving a memoir of her path through resistance to life on its own terms with the letters of her spiritual companion and teacher, the late Brother René of Gethsemani, Colette Lafia invites her reader to practice the spiritual discipline of surrender, the soul's dark path toward a doorway into light, a coming home to accepting—and even in the end loving—life's hard times that bring graces nonetheless."

Jonathan Montaldo
Coeditor of the Bridges to Contemplative Living
with Thomas Merton series

"In this consoling book, Colette Lafia shares with us how a Trappist monk named Brother René helped her to find inner peace by learning to surrender to God, who guides and sustains our lives in mysterious ways we do not understand. Colette shares with us a series of letters in which Brother René marks out the path of sweet surrender that we can follow as we learn to surrender to God's presence in our lives."

James Finley
Former Trappist Monk
Author of *Merton's Palace of Nowhere*

"In her quiet, gentle, and deliberate way, Colette Lafia guides us inexorably toward a juncture most of us try our best to avoid: the place where suffering and surrender meet. If you are in pain, yet long to find God in the midst of it, this is your book."

Paula Huston
Author of *A Land Without Sin*

Seeking Surrender

How My Friendship With a Trappist Monk Taught Me to Trust and Embrace Life

Colette Lafia

SORIN BOOKS / Notre Dame, Indiana

www.sorinbooks.com

Paperback: ISBN-13 978-1-933495-88-0

E-Book: ISBN-13 978-1-933495-89-7

Cover image © Corbis.

Cover and text design by David Scholtes.

Printed and bound in the United States of America.

Library of Congress Cataloging-in-Publication Data

Lafia, Colette.

 Seeking surrender : how my friendship with a Trappist monk taught me to trust and embrace life / Colette Lafia.

    pages cm

 Includes bibliographical references and index.

 ISBN 978-1-933495-88-0 (alk. paper) -- ISBN 1-933495-88-X (alk. paper)

 1. Lafia, Colette--Correspondence. 2. Rene, Brother, -2011--Correspondence. 3. Suffering--Religious aspects--Catholic Church. 4. Spiritual life--Catholic Church. 5. Submissiveness--Religious aspects--Catholic Church. I. Title.

 BX4705.L238A4 2015

 282.092--dc23

 [B]

                    2014045911

To my mother, Gertrude,
in gratitude for all your encouragement
and spiritual friendship.

Contents

Foreword by Daniel P. Horan, O.F.M. xi

Acknowledgments... xv

Introduction: The Threshold xvii

1. An Unexpected Encounter 1

2. A Dialogue in Letters 15

3. Living Surrender 22

4. Remembrance and Reflection 114

5. Learning to Walk the Path of Surrender 123

Notes 135

Foreword

In an age in which we have replaced the quiet, meditative, and anticipatory time of receiving a response to a letter by mail with the instant gratification—and sometimes headache—of near-immediate digital communication, those seeking solitude, peace, and the embrace of the Divine might do well to return to earlier forms of communication.

Prayer is, at its core, simply communication with God. If God is, as St. Augustine famously reminds us, "closer to us than we are to ourselves," then everything we do, say, or think is a form of communication with the Divine. Therefore, communication is expressed in explicit and direct ways through spoken and thought prayers; communication is expressed in silent and reflective ways through meditation and contemplation; and communication is expressed in implicit and subtle ways through our actions and behaviors.

Colette Lafia's journey of prayerful discovery of trust and the embrace of life that is presented in this book unfolds before the reader as an unassuming guide to each of these iterations of communication with God. At the heart of her book is that increasingly endangered earlier form of communication: letter writing. Although the correspondence shared here bears the personal marks of a particular life, with its own struggles and joys, the wisdom exchanged is wonderfully transferable to us all.

Correspondence has long been a spiritual tradition within the Christian community. One need look no further than to the earliest texts contained in the New Testament, that of the epistolary of Saint Paul, to recognize the importance and value of written communication as a form of spiritual inspiration and divine revelation. Saint Paul's first-century Mediterranean audience and their particular concerns may indeed be very different from our twenty-first-century ones. However, the work of the Spirit to continue to inspire women and men millennia later through scripture gives witness to the profound truth that our Christian pilgrimage through life can transcend so many differences, allowing us to draw close to the wisdom and love of God. Colette's letters to and from Brother René reflect this reality. Although her experiences and concerns—the pain of infertility, the loss of a sibling, the aging of a parent, and so on—are unique to her own journey, we can nevertheless see something of our own vulnerability and struggle in her story, just as we can in the particularity of the early Christian communities in Corinth or Philippi or Rome.

In addition to participating in the broader sacred tradition of letter writing within Christianity, Colette and Brother René are also inheritors of a more proximate heritage at the Trappist Abbey of Gethsemani. The religious home of Brother René, not far from Louisville, Kentucky, is also the former home and final resting place of another monk who was deeply committed to the sacred tradition of letter writing. That monk was Fr. M. Louis, better known to the world simply as Thomas Merton. One cannot read Colette's honest missives nor Brother René's wise responses without recalling the decades-long practice of Merton's written correspondence to people all over the world—some very famous, most very ordinary.

On November 10, 1958, in a letter to one very famous person, Pope John XXIII, Merton wrote about how his practice of regular correspondence allowed him to transcend the strictures of the monastery to engage in a form of ministry with people all over the world. His communication with people had allowed him to be present to those who needed kindness and understanding, people of all walks of life and from many different traditions that might benefit personally, intellectually, and spirituality from their written friendship. He wrote, "I have had the experience of seeing that this kind of understanding and friendly sympathy, on the part of a monk who really understands them, has produced striking effects among artists, writers, publishers, poets, etc., who have become my friends without having to leave the cloister." He summarizes his experience, noting, "In short, with the approval of my superiors, I have exercised an apostolate—small and limited though it be—within a circle of intellectuals from other parts of the world; and it has been quite simply an apostolate of friendship."

Half a century later, Brother René carries on the tradition of his brother in religious life by sharing with Colette a true "apostolate of friendship." The wisdom, insight, humor, and vulnerability expressed on both ends help us to enter more deeply and focus more intentionally on our own journey toward surrender. This book is more than a series of reflections and advice, more than a catalog of letters. Like the psalms in the Liturgy of the Hours that Colette came to love and pray after the example of the Trappist monks, these reflections, letters, and helpful methods bear a rhythm that is at once simple and profound.

Daniel P. Horan, O.F.M.
October 4, 2014
Feast of Saint Francis of Assisi

Acknowledgments

I am grateful for the generosity of all those who have been a part of my journey to complete this book. I am infinitely grateful to my husband, Mark, for his unwavering confidence in me and in this project and for the bond of our marriage that keeps strengthening through our life experiences. A big thank you to Leslie Kirk Campbell, an extraordinary writer and teacher, whose guidance, insights, and critical input were so valuable to me in shaping this book. I also extend a warm thank you to Janice Farrell, my spiritual director, for holding this dream with me, and to Suzanne Buckley, director of Mercy Center, for all her encouragement and nurturing. A special thanks to my dear friend Paula Kravitz, for introducing me to Gethsemani and her constant faith in me.

A heartfelt thank you to James Finley for recognizing the heart of my project, believing in it, and helping me to bring it forward. I want to deeply thank Bob Hamma, editorial director of Ave Maria Press, for his trust in this project, and Kristi McDonald, my editor at Ave Maria Press, for her enthusiasm, patience, and support each step of the way.

I thank all those who have touched my life and are a part of this book—my family, my friends, my colleagues, and my spiritual companions—and a special note of gratitude for the friendship I shared with Brother René.

Introduction

The Threshold

It is human nature to strive for what we want and to believe that with hard work, determination, and discipline, we can achieve just about anything. We praise and admire those who accomplish great things, especially in the face of great adversity. Collectively, we hold up perseverance as one of our highest virtues.

But what happens when, despite all our efforts, we don't end up with what we wanted or hoped for, and instead encounter loss, disappointment, and even a sense of failure? Where and how does surrender and acceptance fit into this uncomfortable equation?

The call to surrender arrived in my life unexpectedly and from an unexpected source. On a cool October night in 2002, I found myself standing at the entrance of the Abbey of Gethsemani in rural Kentucky, with my husband at my side, not entirely sure why I had come to a Trappist monastery for a week or what I was even looking for.

After years of having diligently worked to fulfill my dreams for family, work, and personal achievement, I was left with a core experience of emptiness and deep sorrow. My husband and I had not been able to conceive a child and start a family after ten years of trying. My sister had died of breast cancer after three years of treatments, during which I sat by her bedside and cared for the six-year-old daughter she would leave behind. My husband's small communications company was closing after he had put everything he had into the endeavor. And I had developed chronic insomnia, my body dragging through the days like a sack heavy with sand.

I was collapsing, sinking lower than I ever could have imagined. I felt completely dark inside. I cried into the vortex of the universe: *Have mercy on me. . . . Deliver me.* Everything seemed up for question—even God.

I did not know then what it would take for me to come to terms with what had or had not happened in my life. Nor did I know how I could learn to accept the truth of certain limitations of the body, conditions that I was unable to influence or change.

But on my very first day at the Abbey at Gethsemani, I met Brother René, an elderly monk with a warm and down-to-earth disposition, who reached out a hand to welcome me. As our eyes met, the beginning of a more trusting way of being *in* my life and *with* my life unexpectedly appeared.

Brother René would become my spiritual companion, teacher, and a source of inspiration for seven years. Our friendship would eventually shape me, giving me the courage to surrender to the loss and disappointments I had been unable to accept, and awakening in me the faith I so desperately needed. After meeting Brother René, a new path opened up for me, but I had no idea what it was or how to even name it. Now, I can point to it and call it my journey into the heart of surrender, even though at that time, it was just an unknowing, a searching in the dark, and a longing for some light in all the pain.

I had always assumed that surrender meant defeat and resignation. I had placed it in opposition to the more common belief that anything is possible, if only we try hard enough. And yet, beginning with my week at Gethsemani, my own life experience has taught me that neither of these lines of thought measure up to the full reality of our lived experience.

Surrender, I have learned, is neither defeat nor resignation. With Brother René's guidance, I have learned that surrender is the spiritual aspect of acceptance, inviting and allowing us to hold our experiences and lives with grace in every moment. It calls us into a deeper relationship with mystery, with the Divine, and with the force of creation. When it is combined with intention and an open heart, I have found surrender to be the key to transforming grief and pain.

The essence of surrender is trust, but this can be difficult to find at times. It requires us to yield and let the Divine carry us, which can feel like the greatest effort. Although we may land in surrender's lap with a thud, kicking and screaming with resistance, it is, in fact, a soft landing pad. Surrender offers us an embrace, a way to move from grief to grace.

This book is an invitation for you to follow me on my journey of surrender as I navigate my way through infertility; a sleep condition; the loss of my sister; my husband's work hardships; and then later with my father's aging, subsequent struggle with Parkinson's disease, and death.

The genesis of this book was my correspondence with Brother René. The letters we shared became a way for me to become attentive to and discover the path of surrender. Over and over again, the force of resistance tried to overtake me. But through prayer, spiritual direction, painting, journal writing, and my correspondence with Brother René, I began to recognize my resistance and not let it direct me. And the more I became aware of my resistance's shadow, the more I could hear surrender's call.

Though my first steps toward surrender were defined by loss and limitations, the journey opened my eyes, giving me the gift to see beyond the definitions and expectations I had previously set for my life. It was a process of slowly learning to meet life on its own terms and thus moving beyond feelings of betrayal, blame, and regret.

Through this process, I received the grace to allow acceptance and trust to move into the center of my life. I was able to see that I had not reached a dead end but, rather, a crossroads. I was no longer trying to be the controller of my life; I was the receiver.

Over time, I came to realize that surrender is not something to be attained, rather something to be lived. It is not a fixed or absolute state, but a conversation with life and a path that we walk every day. Surrender is a grace we open up to receiving, as well as a practice, one that must be nurtured and cultivated through the choices we make: in how we think, in how we act, and what we hold in our hearts.

I now recognize the call to surrender everywhere: in the way I respond to what each night of sleep may bring, in my daily commitment to my marriage, in how I handle my physical limitations, in my work challenges, in the ways I care for my family, and even in the simplest of things, like how I step into a cool swimming pool and plunge into the water.

Throughout this book, I have woven together my own personal narratives with excerpts from the letters that Brother René and I exchanged over the course of five years. While his words may appear simple and straightforward on the surface, their content and substance are rich. Behind each letter is a lifetime of devotion, reflection, and prayer.

You can read this book by following along chronologically, page to page, or enter anywhere to find a vignette that resonates with you. I have also included *Seeking Surrender* exercises and meditations to encourage and support you along the way.

The *Seeking Surrender* exercises in this book have been invaluable to me in building an awareness and orientation to surrender in my daily experiences. They can also serve as a guide, reminder, or reflection tool for you. Each one of these moments has taught me that letting go is a practice. The more I consent in little ways, the more I can walk, step-by-step, in all areas of my life with an orientation of surrender. These exercises bring the intention of practicing surrender to a more conscious and active level, rather than limiting the notion of surrender to something that is passive.

Living and surrendering are intertwined. I have found that the more we surrender to what is difficult and unwanted, the more we can open up to what is beautiful, profound, and abundant. We stop wanting our lives to be something other than what they are and begin to recognize what is right in front of us, the life that is truly our very own.

I invite you to join me, to take your own journey through the pathway of surrender, and to find what is awaiting you on the other side.

Chapter 1

An Unexpected Encounter

By late summer 2002, my husband and I had been dealing with infertility, cancer, insomnia, and business challenges for more than a decade. We were deeply in love and had been married for fifteen years. But no matter how hard we tried, we could not manifest our long-held dreams for family, work, and personal fulfillment. Instead, our lives were drenched in loss and grief.

Starting a family had proven to be difficult for us. We tried Western medical procedures, acupuncture, and a long list of other methods, but we could not conceive. Every month, we lived through the cycle of anticipation, timing, waiting, and then a deep feeling of letdown when I didn't get pregnant. The months turned into years, and the years soon became a decade. The strong urge in my body to create new life with the man I loved remained unfulfilled. My hope to have my own journey of motherhood, beyond the painful experience of being raised by a mother dealing with alcoholism, seemed to be slipping away.

Meanwhile, after six years of working tirelessly on his communications company, my husband was faced with the fact that his business was not sustainable. Despite the long hours he dedicated to making calls, going to meetings, and completing writing, design, and web projects, he had to accept that he would be forced to close his office.

Underlying these struggles and disappointments, a family tragedy unfolded. One of my older sisters was diagnosed with breast cancer. Over the next three years, as the disease progressed, I cared for her and her family, brushed her thick black hair as it fell out, and experienced the impossible sadness of packing boxes with her journals, pieces of clothing, and photographs for her little girl to have one day. On the day of her funeral, I held her six-year-old daughter's trembling body in my arms.

My heart was broken, and the atmosphere of grief pervading my life intensified. I became acutely aware that anything could happen to the body, and the vulnerability of this truth pressed down heavily on me.

Out of this heaviness, I began to experience insomnia. My nights became unpredictable, as I often found myself awake, unable to fully sleep. My psyche could no longer contain the pressure of handling all I could not control and of holding life and death so closely together. I tried many remedies, but none of them worked well for me. The best I could do was to manage the long and difficult nights. I would listen to meditation tapes, rest on the sofa, cry with frustration, or take a bath.

Together, these circumstances had a cumulative and troubling effect. I felt caged in, unable to influence or control what was going on. I found myself living with layers of loss.

So when a good friend of mine suggested that we get away and spend some time at the Abbey of Gethsemani, a Trappist monastery in rural Kentucky, my husband and I listened. Over the years, she had found solace and spiritual encouragement from spending time with the community of monks that lived there. In need of spiritual support and desperate for some clarity about how to navigate our future, we decided to go. We knew we could not change what had already happened, but *something* needed to change.

We made plans to visit the abbey for a week that same October. Neither my husband nor I knew much about monastic life or the path of a monk. We were not particularly familiar with the writings of the renowned monk and author, Thomas Merton, for whom the monastery was best known. We only knew that we were craving to ease our pain and find a way to live with the unexpected circumstances and tragedies we had faced over the previous decade. I held on to the belief that life had more to offer me than disappointment, sadness, and fatigue.

At the monastery, I hoped to find peace—in the mystical ambience, the chanting, the silence, and the absences of constant striving and worldly desire. I imagined that at Gethsemani I would be able to relinquish all my problems and worries.

My husband and I scraped together the money to go, and under the orange glow of early fall, we traversed the country, traveling by taxi, plane, and car to finally land at this unassuming place with the simple address: Monks Road, Trappist, Kentucky.

Arrival

It was evening when my husband and I arrived in Louis-ville, Kentucky, so we headed straight to the small guest cottage we had rented near the abbey. Finding ourselves unable to settle down and sleep, we got out of bed and drove along the dimly lit, single-lane road to the monastery in time for 3:15 a.m. Vigils. (Monastic life consists of seven periods of communal prayer a day: 3:15 a.m., Vigils; 5:45 a.m., Lauds; 7:30 a.m., Terce; 12:15 p.m., Sext; 2:15 p.m., None; 5:30 p.m., Vespers; and 7:30 p.m., Compline.)

It was a clear and crisp October night, with the rural Kentucky sky brimming with stars. The monastery was easy to find, being the only building on a long stretch of empty road. We pulled into the parking lot and followed the walkway that led into a compound of buildings. We found our way into the stone church, taking seats in the assigned section along with a handful of other guests, who, like us, were bundled in sweaters and wearing sleepy looks.

We watched the hooded monks arrive in the silence of the night, tucked deeply into themselves. For the next half hour, they chanted the psalms in English, recited prayers, sat in silence for a while, and then stood up in unison and filed out of the church. As we drove back to our cottage, I had an intense feeling of doubt. The simple Shaker-style of the church along with the monotonous sound of the monks singing the psalms in English left me uninspired. My romantic image of a monastery shattered. I didn't have the feeling that these monks, who had renounced the world, were being swept away into some celestial transcendence.

Around noon later that same day, we headed back to the monastery, which I could now see was set among open fields of tall grass and rolling hills. With only a few hours of sleep, I was tired and in a funk. "What are we doing here?" I asked my husband, as we trudged up the walkway to the hospitality center. "We're here to meet some monks," he said with a smile. I was hesitant but followed him up the stairs. I knew that the only direction for me at this point was forward, so I kept moving, even with my doubts.

As soon as we entered the abbey's reception area, I felt more at ease. There were several monks in their black-and-white robes, smiling and mingling with the guests in an atmosphere that was warm and welcoming. They were keeping alive the rule of Saint Benedict, the founder of monastic life, who in the sixth century wrote: "Let all guests who arrive be received as Christ, because He will say: 'I was a stranger and you took Me in.'"

We walked over to the reception desk, where we were greeted by a friendly older monk. We introduced ourselves. This was Brother René. He looked to be in his seventies. He had perfectly straight posture and a broad smile accentuated his high cheekbones. He spoke in a calm, even tone and moved at a steady pace. I noticed the deliberateness in his gesture as he handed me the daily schedule of meal times and prayer periods.

He told us about the nearby hiking trails, the evening talks in the chapel, and the bookstore in a nearby building. We chatted about where we were from, and I also asked him a few questions about himself.

I discovered he was of French-Canadian ancestry and from New England, which, coincidentally, was similar to my grandmother's heritage. I also discovered he would be celebrating his fiftieth anniversary as an ordained monk during the upcoming weekend and that a special jubilee Mass would be taking place to mark the occasion. I was struck by this detail, since my parents had recently celebrated their marriage of fifty years, and I realized it was a lifetime.

As my husband looked at some maps at a nearby table, I continued talking with Brother René. He asked me more about myself, and I told him about my work in education and about being married for fifteen years and not yet having children. "It's been difficult," I said. "I'll keep you both in my prayers," he replied. I softly thanked him and prepared to leave.

We were silent while I gathered up the various schedules and information, and then, on impulse, I leaned slightly forward into the desk dividing us, looked up at him, and unequivocally asked: "Are you ever lonely?"

He paused for a moment, gazing down at his folded hands. I stood still, and to my own surprise, I did not feel compelled to explain or justify my question. In truth, I had no idea why I would ask such a thing at that moment. He looked back up at me with his kind brown eyes and simply said, "No, just as you have had a companion in your husband all these years, I have had a constant companion in God."

I didn't say anything back in response but only received his words. In that moment, the gulf between us seemed to close, and we were held together in a place of grace. Little did I know that this monk would become my teacher and that I would learn from him how to respond with greater trust and confidence to the difficult circumstances of my life.

Within the first day of arriving at the abbey, the new path I had been seeking opened up, almost imperceptibly, without my even realizing it. All around the monastery, the fall leaves were changing from shades of green to golden yellow and burnt orange. And there I was, turning with them, changing from one season of my life to another.

Immersion

My husband and I gradually acclimated to the rhythm and pace of Gethsemani. I attended most of the daily prayer periods, ate my meals in silence in the guest cafeteria, took slow walks on the grounds, and sat quietly in the garden while writing in my journal. My husband met with some of the monks who made themselves available to the guests: one was a published poet and another was a charismatic monk who gave daily evening talks that weaved together his stories of sailing, pieces of literature, and nuggets of spiritual wisdom.

I soon found solace in the church. The interior had been renovated in the Shaker style, with simple crossbeam arches, birch-wood pews, and white walls. There were no large crosses, no paintings on the walls, and no sizable statues or ornamentation. Only a small wooden statue of Mary was displayed, the honored Mother of Gethsemani, with the illumination of one candle placed beneath her. Here, she watched over all of us.

The walls of the church held a silence I could feel in my bones. I liked it. Its weight was interior and had a different measure. At the monastery, I began to notice my tension between surrendering and resisting. In my interior storm I was like that candle flickering, taking shelter in the stone church. I felt the light in God, in myself, seeking union. *God a verb. Bringing forth.* Not a blazing fire or a bolt of lightning but a small voice, craving a listening that was carved, a listening that required silence to be heard.

The presence of the monks, along with the steady sound of their voices blending in unison as they chanted the psalms during prayer, was encouraging. As I looked over at the entrance to the monks' quarters, where the sign above it read "God Alone," I felt a nudging inside of me, something stirring and inviting me in.

During the week, Brother René and I exchanged words only sporadically and briefly. I was prepared for this, since when I asked him about the monks' vow of silence, he informed me that at Gethsemani they were permitted to speak but only with intention and purpose, as they did when assigned to the reception desk or to offer hospitality to the guests.

Yet even without talking frequently, I felt a palpable connection to him. I was aware of his presence as he took his place in the pews for the daily prayers, and when we gathered in the small chapel to recite the Rosary, or as the guests and monks walked through the church courtyard together in silence after the evening Compline. Often, he would glance over at me, and we would exchange a look of recognition, a nod, or a soft smile.

The monastic way of life at Gethsemani intrigued me. During the day, we rarely saw most of the monks. They were busy living the Benedictine philosophy of work and prayer. They prepared meals for the guests and the community and took care of the grounds. They made cheese, fudge, and fruitcake in their workshops to fulfill orders from their online store in order to keep the monastery self-sufficient—truly the medieval meeting the modern.

After a few days into our week-long stay, I began to notice that while the monks always entered the church for prayer dressed in the signature black-and-white robe, it was each monk's favorite footwear that stood out as his most distinguishing and recognizable feature. These devoted monks expressed their individuality with their shoes: Birkenstock, Clark, Ecco, Rockport, and Timberland.

One afternoon, my husband and I sat under a two-hundred-year-old Ginkgo tree in the heart of the monastery's garden, enjoying a conversation with one of the monks who was a poet. We talked about a range of things, from the variety of human emotions expressed in the psalms, to the need for the monks to wear good shoes in order to stand and walk on the stone floors of the monastery. He told us that the monks used to wear donated shoes, but because of the intensity of their backaches from standing and walking on these floors, they were now permitted to order shoes from various catalogues.

"What kind of shoes are those?" he asked me, staring intently at my suede brown loafers. "Maybe I should try a pair."

I told him I would send him a catalog, which I later did. Who knew how important shoes would be for a life of devotion!

On the third day of our visit, I was overcome with fatigue as I continued to struggle with insomnia during my nights at the guest cottage. I sat in the church as the dawn appeared through the small square windows, casting its pink light on the stone wall. While saying the morning prayers, all I could focus on was the heaviness in my legs and my aching lower back. I felt just like the monks with their backaches. Here I was, wanting to reach beyond myself, and all I could focus on was my strained and tired body.

After Mass, I remained in the church among the monks who were sitting in silence, with the cowls of their white morning robes covering their heads. Since my sweater also had a hood, I imitated the monks and pulled it over my head, creating a cave for myself. *God, I am stripping away all my images of you, and I don't know what is left. I just don't understand any of it,* I prayed.

As I sat quietly, I was drawn into my body, weary from not sleeping well and from all the effort and difficulty of the past years. I closed my eyes and leaned back into the wooden pew, absorbing the energy of the monks around me steeped in prayer.

With each breath, I sank more into the early morning silence, and deeper into my body, until my breathing seemed to form a union with the atmosphere around me. I felt a seamless connection between myself, the monks, and the presence of God. As I absorbed this moment, I sensed the tender touch of divine love in me, so gentle and full of compassion. I did not have to get away from myself but, rather, I needed to get closer to myself. The seeds of surrender were opening in the intimacy of this deep, interior listening.

Here at the monastery, my prayers began to change. My internal litany started to fade away, and I welcomed more emptiness. The heavy weight inside of me began to lift, allowing some light to penetrate the density. The monks and guests created a force of prayer that formed a strong and sturdy net, holding all who came searching, all who arrived with a need. I was in the right place.

One evening, after the night prayer, as the monks were leaving the church on their way back to their quarters, Brother René came over to me in the courtyard. He handed me some folded papers.

"I wanted to share my notes for the talk I plan to give to the community as part of my jubilee," he said, referring to his golden anniversary as a Trappist monk to be celebrated at the abbey over the weekend.

"Thank you," I said.

"My talk is based on the conversation we had when we first met," he added. "Please slip the papers under the door of the hospitality office when you are finished."

I held the loose sheets securely in my hands. We said good night, and I watched Brother René's black robe become a silhouette as he walked to his room. The night air brushed against my cheeks. I stood still for a few minutes, struck by this gesture of trust. I had come here for me, seeking answers for my life, and yet, I had touched the life of this monk preparing for his milestone. I looked up at the stars with an overwhelming sense that there was a pattern to what I was seeing, even if I did not know what it was.

The next morning, I sat in the monastery garden and pulled out the papers I had stored safely in my journal. I scanned the handwritten words filling the pages, deeply moved that I was being brought into such a private experience. I began to slowly read Brother René's words:

In my years at Gethsemani I was not lonely, because I have not been alone. You, God, were my companion in

life. We went to choir together and in the refractory we
sat next to each other. At work in the barn, there was only
You and I as we talked through the day. And the meals I
cooked were for You. When I worked in the garden and
gave advice to the novices, it was You I was speaking
to. . . . Love is the force, the common bond of our life in
God, for God is love.

The pages overflowed with his awareness and gratitude
for the presence of God infused in the daily moments of
his fifty years in the monastery.

I felt quiet inside, absorbing the intimacy of the
moment and savoring his words. I took out my travel-size
watercolor set, dipped the small brush into my water bot-
tle, and in my journal created a few quick paintings of the
garden. What was Brother René doing at this moment, I
wondered? I imagined his companionship with God filling
him with peace and joy.

Later that day, when I slipped his notes underneath the door of the hospitality office, I included one of
my watercolors with a note of thanks, letting him know
how much his writing touched me. I now recognized the
mystery and gift in our meeting even more. I wrote in
my notebook: "All I know is something has touched me
deeply—more deeply than I can understand at this point."

That Sunday, the day of Brother René's celebration,
the church was filled with people from the surround-
ing community attending Mass, along with the monks,
the retreatants and guests, and Brother René's sister and

brother, whom he had introduced me to in the morning. I sat in a pew toward the front so I could see the altar. My husband was beside me, quietly observing everything.

I watched intently as Brother René prostrated himself in his white robe on the bare stone floor of the church. His outstretched arms and straight body formed the shape of a cross. It was the same posture he had taken when he accepted the life of a monk fifty years before, and now, he fully inhabited it.

I was drawn to this compelling image of surrender. My eyes softened with tender tears. The melodic prayers and songs of the community permeated the church and filled me. I could sense I had been led here, that this juncture in my life would be a defining one.

Return

Our week at the monastery soon came to a close, and it was time to go home. I somehow knew my time there had been a turning point. When we returned to San Francisco, my husband and I agreed we would try one last treatment to conceive. I wrote to Brother René and asked him to pray for us as we faced this uncertainty. He wrote back within a week, and thus began our dialogue that would last for many years, about surrender, hope, faith, mystery, loss, God, and the power of love.

Chapter 2

A Dialogue in Letters

It has been more than a month since we have returned from Gethsemani, and images of the monastery and the monks linger in my mind. I can still see Brother René's kind eyes and feel his warmth. Early one Saturday morning, I sit at my desk in our second bedroom, looking out the window at the orange streaks in the sky from the sunrise. I am sipping my tea and preparing to write in my journal, which has become my morning ritual. My husband is still sleeping. Since our return, we have been to the fertility specialist and made arrangements for our upcoming treatment. I have no words left inside of me about this. I just hold a silent hope.

As I am flipping through my journal, I find this note that I had written about Brother René while staying at Gethsemani:

He was waiting for a message. I was the messenger. He wasn't really expecting me. I wasn't expecting him. Perhaps he thought I was sent by Mary, the holy Mother.

And perhaps I believed that, too. In a moment of sacred connection, I was the missing piece he was seeking. Mary was softly whispering to me. Her devoted servant, Brother René, was listening, listening in the silence of his heart—waiting for the right words to express the moment of his fiftieth anniversary at Gethsemani.

After I read this, I feel compelled to switch on the computer and compose my first letter to Brother René. The words come quickly, while a few tears softly stream down my cheeks. Yes, I can sense this was right. It is a short note, and I don't rewrite any of the words. I print it, put it in a white envelope, find the address of the monastery, and mail it that afternoon, not knowing what to expect.

December 6, 2002
Dear Brother René,

I have thought of you often and of the small miracle of sharing the weekend of your fiftieth celebration. I am grateful for my time at Gethsemani. As I mentioned to you, my husband and I have been trying to have a child for many years and it has been difficult for us. We have decided to have one last medical procedure in hope of conceiving. We ask that you keep us in your prayers during this time.

Most of all, I am praying to trust my life and for my faith to become stronger not weaker through my trials and experiences. During my time at Gethsemani, I began to sense my need and desire to surrender, to let go and depend on divine grace more. But it is not easy for me.

Warmly,
Colette

A week later, I find a letter in my mailbox postmarked Monk's Road, Kentucky. I set the envelope on the table next to the armchair in my bedroom. It is only later, after my husband and I have had dinner and cleaned up, that I can settle into my chair with an uninterrupted moment to open it. I carefully slip my index finger under the triangular flap and pull out the thin sheets of paper. Holding them gently between my two hands, I begin to read the words that have traveled more than a thousand miles to reach me.

December 11, 2002
Dear Colette,
Peace. Joy. Love.

Thank you for your letter and be assured of our prayers. I will put a note on the board for all to join me in remembering your intention. Your letter stirred up many emotions in me. As a boy, my ambition was to get married and raise a big family. God has answered my prayer in a way different than I expected when he gave me the desire to enter the monastery.

Believe me, God will answer your prayer, but it's not for me to know how or when. Trust that He will answer in the way that is best for you and Mark. I do believe in medical treatments too because God works through them to help us. Your words about praying for an increase in trust and faith are ideal. Now do it! God will not fail you.

Let me take the occasion of my letter to thank you for the lovely drawing and message for my jubilee. Meeting you and your husband Mark was a blessing in my life for an insight you gave to me when we discussed loneliness.
United in Prayer,
In His Love,
Brother René

A month later, I write to Brother René again, and the rhythm to our dialogue begins to get established.

January 13, 2003
Dear Brother René,

Your letter touched me deeply. I reached out and shared such a private and painful situation, and you gave me so much respect and love in return. Our medical treatment to conceive failed, which has been extremely painful for us. At first I cried to God, asking: Why? Why can't I have just one child? I felt so much grief and confusion. But as the weeks have passed, I have been able to turn back toward God, returning to your words that God will not fail us and knows what is best for me and Mark.

I pray now for deeper faith, to trust and surrender to what I cannot understand. I don't know what direction my life is going in right now, whether I will pursue adoption or choose to live without children. In some ways, Mark and I are facing rebuilding our lives from the collapse of the last decade. How do I listen to God now?

I am so grateful to know that you are praying for me. I feel less alone. I hope you are well and that God's peace continues to comfort you.

Warmly,

Colette

Just six days later, I find a letter from Brother René in my mailbox. His letters, I notice, are always handwritten with a black or blue ballpoint pen. He isn't self-conscious about crossing out a phrase or inserting a missing word. What he cares about is what he is saying, not the presentation. Sometimes, he even draws a smiley face after a sentence to emphasize a statement or adds several exclamation points.

I find myself reading his letter three or four times, penetrating the meaning of the words with each reading. Often I cry not because the letters are particularly emotional but from an overwhelming sense of relief that I am being heard.

January 19, 2003

Dear Colette,

Thank you for your lovely letter. Do not give up hope. You may remember my saying that my desire was to get married and raise a big family. Then I prayed for the grace to know God's will and to do it, and was answered with a vocation to come to Gethsemani.

Here I find my desires answered. I cannot say how your prayers will be answered, but I am confident that they will be.

You ask how to listen to God in your life. Well, I often write dialogues by which I have learned to listen to my deeper self and what I believe God is asking of me. Writing poetry or even a daily journal does the same thing for some people who want to learn the art of listening. A movement of the heart is foremost among the signs and ways of knowing if what one hears is inspired by the Spirit. There is the experience of peace and of quiet satisfaction. So I will end on this note and will continue remembering you both in prayer.
In His Love,
Brother René

Writing my letters and receiving his letters becomes an essential part of my life. In this intimate exchange, I am whispering across pieces of paper, trying to make sense of what confounds me and listen to what resides in my heart. The voice of this monk speaks back to me from the scratches of his pen, a man who has lived most of his life in a monastery, rising in the middle of the night for prayer, walking down the long corridor of his mind, until he enters a quieter room, where he hears the language of his own heart.

I begin to realize that surrender is not an entirely new concept to me. I grew up with images and teachings of it in the Catholic Church, and I also heard my mother speak about it during her recovery process from alcoholism. I was in high school when she had entered a rehabilitation center for thirty days and stopped drinking. Her journey was one of surrendering, as I witnessed her going to AA meetings, starting therapy, and attending Mass regularly. I watched my parents repair their marriage with faith and forgiveness, patching a roof that had been leaking for a long time.

Even so, the notion was never as personal as it has now become through my fledgling correspondence with Brother René. Our letters start to cultivate the sense of surrender I first felt stirring in me during my week at Gethsemani: its essence, its teaching, its seeking. A narrow door begins to open to a God I cannot contain, asking me to step inside and come closer.

I decide to save our letters. It becomes a ritual for me, to place each piece of loose paper into a clear sheet protector and add it to my collection in a white three-ring binder, with a photograph of Brother René and me on the cover, taken in front of the abbey. I keep the letters in chronological order, and every time I add a new one, I am aware of the spiritual companionship that Brother René and I are sharing through our dialogue.

I recognize that our most significant relationships often start mysteriously, of their own accord. I met my husband in a passing moment at a coat check in a café on a cold winter's night in Montreal. And I met Brother René on a fall afternoon at a hospitability desk, in a fleeting moment, when we recognized something in each other. What, I wondered, does this friendship want to offer me?

Chapter 3

Living Surrender

Morning

My husband and I do not know what to expect. Each morn-ing, we sit together and have breakfast, grateful for this simple ritual. We eat fresh fruit and pieces of toast, and we drink English breakfast tea with milk. My husband's slender frame leans into the pine table, as his hazel eyes, soft in the waking hours, scan the online newspaper, while I usually write in my journal. There is a great love holding us together—stronger than our deflated spirits.

We are a married couple without children. From the outside, we look like an ordinary pair, tending to the daily necessities of life. We ride our bicycles through Golden Gate Park, buy food at the local farmer's market, and go to work—my husband in his small communications busi-ness and myself providing professional development for teachers. We take care of our home. We spend time with family and friends. But from the inside, my husband and

I have traveled the distance of our souls, through long, dark nights.

Now, a few months after our week at Gethsemani and the conclusion of our final treatment to conceive, we step into a new passage, mixed with sadness, loss, faith, and a desire to find some relief. Together, we see that surrender is another choice. We stop trying to make our lives into what we wanted them to be, and instead receive what they are. There have been no shortcuts to arrive at this moment—we have met loss, sat with death, and faced the certainty of not having what we longed for.

Several years ago, when we were visiting family in Canada, my mother-in-law casually remarked that my husband and I must be used to being without children after all these years. Something in me snapped. I rushed into the hallway bathroom, locked the door, and gave in to a flood of tears.

She knocked. "I'm sorry," she said. "I didn't mean to upset you."

When my husband returned from running an errand, we sat together on the sofa, leaning into each other. His mother was crying her own tears for not having the chance to become a grandmother. Together we shared another layer of the loss.

In his next letter, Brother René encloses a prayer by Thomas Merton from his book *Thoughts in Solitude*. The words resonate:

My Lord God, I have no idea where I am going. I do
not see the road ahead of me. I cannot know for certain
where it will end. . . . Therefore I will trust you always
though I may seem to be lost and in the shadow of
death.[1]

Our day begins with breakfast. We stay faithful to
the journey, faithful to each other. Compassion fills the
air, along with the sweet fragrance of fresh strawberries
on the table. Marriage is different than we expected; work
is different than we expected; we are different than we
expected. We no longer want to impose ourselves onto the
life we imagined for ourselves but, rather, bend as trees do
in the wind, into what *is*.

We are beginning. It's a gradual, day-by-day process.
We allow love to expand, to reach beyond expectations.

―――――――――――//―――――――――――

Seeking Surrender

Give voice to your desire to let go of something. In your
journal, write the following sentence: "I want to let go of . . ."

You may have a specific situation, feeling, or recurring thought that is calling to be released. Write for as long
as you need to, or do a series of journal entries over a week
using the same writing prompt. Be willing to express the
depth and range of your feelings. Trust that listening to
your inner voice is a sacred and holy process, creating the
receptive ground for surrender.

―――――――――――//―――――――――――

Within Water

In the deep waters of uncertainty, I hear Brother René's words: "Do not give up hope." What could this possibly mean for me—a woman in her forties, living without the children she had desired to birth, without her beloved sister, without the security of steady income, and who, at the end of a long day, cannot even count on a good night's sleep?

I need to feel hope in my body.

Swimming has become one of my ways of hoping. When I am immersed in the water, I no longer feel separate from what surrounds me, and in this union, I reconnect with my spirit.

I have been swimming for as long as I can remember, first in a public pool, then in the shimmering, green Atlantic Ocean, and now in a university Olympic-sized pool. As I steadily move up and down the narrow lanes, I modulate my breath, surrendering to the rhythm of my strokes. The water seeps into my skin, covers my face, changing how I hear and the way I see.

When swimming, I am always in the divine presence. I flow within the water, letting go into what holds me. Here, I find freedom and release, whether I am floating on the surface or plunging into the depth.

I swim like I pray, by connecting the body and breath. It is a holy experience for me, and I talk about this with my spiritual director, who is trained to listen to and support others along their spiritual paths. We sit in her cozy office located on the ground floor of her home, in two cloth-covered chairs. We talk about the sacred dimension of my everyday life, which includes my commitment to swimming and the feeling of hope I get when I am moving with ease in the water.

On one visit, my spiritual director pulls a silver frame off her bookshelf and shows me a black-and-white photograph of an Olympic diver in midair, in the graceful arc of a back dive. His arms are raised like open wings, as he eloquently drops back toward the water. The grace and freedom of the dive reminds me of Brother René, with his open arms, prostrate on the church floor during his jubilee Mass.

"That is surrender," I exclaim, staring at the picture.

I imagine letting go with a high diver's sense of confidence and release, boldly springing off the diving board with complete faith.

> February 16, 2003
> Dear Brother René,
>
> I see that this time is a call to trust. Must I let new desire fill my heart, even though I carry the risk of disappointment after so many years of crying out, pleading, begging, praying for a child?
>
> When my sister had breast cancer, I also prayed with all my heart that she would heal and stay alive to care for her daughter. But she died. How do I open my heart and trust in what will be? I don't want to have a child's

relationship to God. I don't want to ask for what I want and then feel betrayed if it doesn't happen.

Is trust in God also a deeper trust in myself?

Warmly,
Colette

February 25, 2003
Dear Colette,
Peace. Joy. Love.

Thank you for your letter and the watercolor drawing. Where you are right now is the only place you can start.

You did not get the answer you were looking for when your sister died to this world. But instead of digging for answers, we need to go heavenward and plunge forth with love, hope, and confidence to wherever God will lead. Yes, let go of that inner fear. It is my prayer that you see what I see. You do have a deep relationship with God that is obvious, and it's not a child's relationship. Yet, still we must go deeper and deeper. Trusting and trusting.

To think of only a physical child is to put limits on God. Can I say expand the concept of what your desires are? The child that God gives you may be a work of love (of whatever kind) but it will be your child and you will be at peace. What is at the core here is your relationship with God. A mother experiences her baby as an extension of herself. God is mother. You are a baby. You are God's extension in time.

United in Prayer,

In His Love,
Brother René
P.S. We will be on retreat next week. Remember us in
prayer as we absorb His Love in order to share it.

Holding On

There is an absolute silence to insomnia. The houses around
me are still and dark, while my husband is sound asleep.

I write in my journal:

> I'm up in the middle of the night. Dear God, do you hear
> me? I am so angry and discouraged right now. The insomnia
> has escalated. I am in another cycle of stormy nights. I don't
> know where to turn. Where are you? Why, why, why—all
> the whys are nothing. I need you.

I expected to get over the insomnia years ago, but
after trying many different remedies and approaches, I
continue to face difficult periods when I cannot sleep with
ease. It takes fortitude, faith, and, as my father would often
say, "Perseverance," but how long must I persevere?

My sleeplessness is often activated by feelings of
grief. I see my niece growing up without my sister, her
father now remarried, living in a different apartment with
a caring stepmother and a new baby sister. The boxes
my sister and I packed with her belongings are stored in
my brother's basement, waiting for my niece when she
becomes a young woman.

My sister's death is a shadow that accompanies us at holiday gatherings and birthday parties. Every year I tell my niece the story about the day she was born and the happiness and fulfillment she brought to her mother. And every year, on her birthday, she looks forward to hearing that story.

Inside the darkness of the night, I meet myself, alone, without the usual armor covering me—the responsible employee, the committed wife, the faithful daughter, the helpful friend, or the reliable sister. I find myself with disheveled hair, wearing flannel pajamas and an old black cashmere sweater, torn at the elbows. I lie on the sofa, the sound of my heart beating strongly in my ears, and watch the moonlight behind the bamboo blinds. Once again, I am facing the uncertainty of the night.

And yet, I sense that I am not alone. I remember Brother René's fifty years at Gethsemani and his constant companionship with God. I pray to trust and to release into what holds me in the darkness. It is not easy. Fear waits around the edges, but my breath provides an anchor as I inhale love and exhale love, feeling its power inside of me. A softness envelops me, and within the silence, I find a place to wait and hold on.

-------------------//-------------------

Seeking Surrender

Connecting with your breath more consciously can be a spiritual tool to help you hold on and find stability in the darker moments. Try the following method: Place one hand on your abdomen and your other hand on your chest. Breathe in and out, feeling the breath in your body. Don't worry if your breath seems choppy at first. It will find its own rhythm. Stay with it, even if you experience frustration, tears, busy thoughts, or the impulse to get up. Let the soft weight of your hands and the movement of your breath anchor you and embrace you.

———————————⫶———————————

Being Shaped

I walk through the Rodin sculpture galleries at the Legion of Honor museum in San Francisco. The rooms are filled with bulging forms of human figures and faces emerging from plaster, marble, and bronze. The natural light that streams in from the high ceilings makes the pieces seem alive. When I look closely at each one, I notice the imprint of the artist's fingers in the bumpy and uneven surfaces, as though the works are still in the process of creation.

I feel like one of these sculptures. The image of God as the potter and us as the clay comes to mind. I am in creation and of creation, being formed beyond my own image of myself. In communion with these dynamic forms, I sense we are molded by the interplay of life and grace.

I see a similar shaping in my father, in the way his personal story lives in the creases of his olive skin, the contours of his rounded shoulders, and the thickness of his hands and fingers. It is all there—his work as a surgeon, his conversion to Catholicism, his fifty-year marriage, the demands of raising a large family, his passion for reading, and the recent years of coping with Parkinson's disease.

I also witnessed the evidence of this sculpting on the cover of the invitation to my parents' fiftieth wedding anniversary, which occurred five years before Brother René's jubilee celebration. The printed card had two parallel photographs on the front: a black-and-white one of the newlyweds in their twenties, with dark hair, broad shoulders, and eager smiles, alongside a color photograph of the couple in their later years, both with gray hair, soft cheeks, and smiling in a quiet way, with less insistence. Here, I see how time, how life, and how grace have carved them through the years.

I am catching glimpses of the way life shapes us, of the way the Divine is kneading us, of the way creation is formed. Standing in the gallery, surrounded by Rodin's art, I understand that one receives life rather than controls it. To surrender is to allow ourselves to be the raw material in the Sculptor's hand.

March 20, 2003
Dear Brother René,

Your advice for me to stop digging is good, because understanding can come in another way, from contemplation, and not always from striving for answers. To look heavenward is to turn in the direction of faith. I am asking God: What direction do I go in now? My heart is slowly opening and becoming more receptive, as I continue to pray.

It's strange after all these years to stop looking for solutions and allow something to be at rest. Can I yield to the feeling of the wind on my cheeks? Can I allow my prayers to expand? Can I, as you said in your letter, go deeper and deeper, trusting and trusting?

Thank you for your support and being a spiritual friend through this time of searching and questioning.

Warmly,

Colette

March 26, 2003

Dear Colette,

To dig is to find rational answers to our problems. But many times, we will never really know the true answers. We can only guess. God just wants us to use our will and have faith that God is and will act through us and others.

It is good that you are praying. Because you are married, you have a wonderful way of knowing just how you are doing in your prayer life. Mark will sense that you are more loving. He will be drawn to love you more and more and will feel secure in your love for him.

I thank God for using me to help you in these matters. It brings strength and joy into my life, and I thank you for opening your heart. I feel God speaking to me through you and for this I am grateful. Hah! There are some good things in life if we let them happen.

United in Prayer,

Brother René

Sacred Engagement

With Brother René's prompting, I begin to pay more attention to my prayer life. I find different practices to encourage me, such as meditation, reciting the Rosary, reading spiritual texts, listening to sacred music, keeping a spiritual journal, and participating in rituals, such as going to Mass.

I discover that prayer is dynamic, and there are many ways to be in relationship with the Spirit moving within me and all around me. I pray as I walk in nature—listening to the ocean waves, smelling the pine trees, or feeling the weight of my feet touching the ground. I say prayers of gratitude throughout my day, being thankful for time to swim, for the meals I eat, and for the comfort of my home and the companionship of my husband.

I remember that when I was a child, I would kneel, recite prayers, and secretly talk to God. I enjoyed this special relationship. But my family was always arguing about religion. Being a convert from Judaism to Catholicism, my father had the need to justify his decision to his belligerent brothers, and then later to his rebellious sons, who constantly challenged his adopted faith. As a result, I turned inward, and my spiritual life became more of an interior journey, not one filled with the pressure to defend the truth but one of following a loving path.

Since my trip to Gethsemani, I have paid more attention to finding the Divine in my day-to-day life. The monks do not separate the routine of daily life from their spiritual life, and I yearn for the same perspective. I find prayer offers me a way to dwell in the depth of my experience. It creates a spiritual context for my life, while at work, or while I swim, or as I engage in daily conversations and concerns.

I keep praying, even when at times my mind gets stuck on repetitive habits of discontent and worry, like a piece of music looping around the same few notes. I keep praying, when all I can say is: *Show me the way, God. I can't find it on my own.* I keep praying even when my prayers are not answered in the way I want them to be answered. And somehow, through my meandering and my commitment, I find a tender resting place in my heart for surrender to make a home.

Seeking Surrender

What is an image of prayer for you? Choose an object that symbolizes prayer for you. It could be anything, a rock, a seed, a shell, a Rosary, a photograph—whatever calls to you. Place the object on your lap or on a table and reflect on how it represents prayer for you. For example, you might choose a seed because a seed represents new growth and possibility, and prayer is about awakening something in you. You might select a bowl because the act of prayer reminds you of the need to give and receive. Take time to write in your journal about your object and your insight, for this too is prayer. Remember that personal images are powerful and can guide you in your spiritual journey.

———————————————//———————————————

Shades of Love

On the weekends, my husband and I ride our bikes through Golden Gate Park near our house. Often, we put on our backpacks and head through the park to a local farmer's market.

Today, while I am riding, I feel the fresh air brush against my cheeks, and my spirit comes alive as I pedal along the path. I ride past oak trees, eucalyptus trees, open fields of bright grass, blooming flowers, and rows of rose bushes. Shades of green flicker in the sunlight under a pure, blue sky.

All that is alive around me pulses through my blood.

Then, in a flash, a wave of hesitation comes over me. Riding along a dirt trail, I feel my tires bouncing over the bumpy and rocky surface. I become aware that I could hit a protruding rock or a fallen branch and lose my balance on the uneven terrain. I begin to tighten up. *But is it possible,* I wonder, *to continue to be at ease and not to grip my handlebars, not to worry about the possibility of falling?*

I recognize the fear, and I decide to focus my attention back to the joy of riding my bike. I slow down a little and stay aware of my surroundings. In doing so, I move closer to the present moment, rather than further away into worrying about what might be. I feel my breath take in the cool air. I hear birds chirping. I notice the shadows of the trees dancing across the open field. I stay with what is really happening and do not get lost in the corners of my mind.

Ahead of me, I see my husband gliding down the trail. He turns back to see where I am. I smile. I open myself to the freedom of the wind and the beauty of the foliage around me. Surrender allows me to let go of fear, to open up and to receive what is offered in the moment—bringing love forward.

April 12, 2003
Dear Brother René,

Greetings and may God's love fill you with joy! Today is my sixteenth wedding anniversary. I am so grateful for my union with Mark, and yes, just as you have said, my marriage is a wonderful way of knowing just how I am doing in my prayer life. It is in my daily life that I see the fruits of prayer, and how I am giving and receiving love.

These days, I am very drawn to praying the Liturgy of the Hours. So many feelings are expressed in the psalms. They are a deep source of contemplation for me. What I find is most important right now is to stay faithful to prayer and nurture my relationship with God. More and more I am bringing my whole self to God.

I wish you a joyful Easter. Thank you for your prayers. I can feel them. They are touching my heart. Many times, thoughts of you come to me and I smile.
In God's love and friendship,
Colette

May 13, 2003

Dear Colette,

Thank you for your lovely Easter card and remembrance. Greetings to Mark. How wonderful to have your anniversary over Easter. Your meeting and relationship with Mark is God's gift. Your relationship with him will never be in competition with your relationship with God. You will find God in him and he will find God in you.

It is good that you are drawing toward prayer and especially the Liturgy of the Hours. The psalms are filled with our human experiences and emotions. But it's important not to take them literally. Always pray the psalms in a way that gives glory to a loving God. Still you must realize we all change. There will be times when you will be drawn to some other form of prayer.

Be aware that what you experience is God's life in you. Yes, it is God's work and action. What matters is giving time to prayer and keeping our hearts open to love however God wills it.

In His Love,

Brother René

Wide Spaces

In yoga class, I raise my arms to a T shape, but tightness limits my movement. The instructor comes over and says, "You can reach out farther than that." She places her open palm in the middle of my back and pushes into it gently.

As she does, my chest lifts, allowing my arms to extend still farther.

This shift, from limitation to possibility, happens in a moment—from a movement in the body, from a choice of words in a conversation, or even from catching a recurring thought and not letting it run wild. The slight change allows me to find the open window behind the closed curtains. Such subtle shifts are sometimes barely visible, but they are present if I pay attention.

In this brief experience during yoga class, my body becomes my teacher. I feel the soles of my feet on the cool hardwood floor, and in the next pose, I lift my arms straight up over my head. I allow my chest to broaden, directing my energy toward what is available rather than toward what is restricting me. In this expansion, I am opening myself to possibility.

"We always look for the windows of opening in the body," my instructor reminds me. I realize I don't have to force the effort but, rather, receive it. I don't have to push into surrender but, rather, release into its spaciousness.

Seeking Surrender

Find a place to sit quietly: in your car, on a chair at home, or on a park bench. Now, breathe in and out. Pay attention to your breath, and begin to scan your body. Slowly move your awareness from your head to your feet—the eyes, the jaw, the shoulders, the arms, the chest, the back, the

legs, and the feet. Notice if there are any areas where you
are holding on too tightly. Perhaps there is a strain in your
eyes, a thickness in your throat, or a tightness in your back.
After a while, let your attention rest on one area. Use the
gentleness of the breath to keep you focused, and stay with
this for three to five minutes. When you finish, notice how
you feel. Did any thoughts or feelings come up for you in
the process? Let your body be your teacher.

Inside the Music

I witness my father physically declining from old age and
from Parkinson's disease. He moves around his house
with the aid of a walker. I watch him clutching the metal
apparatus with his trembling hands as he lifts himself out
of his dining-room chair. His legs often freeze. "Legs, do
your thing," I hear him call out to them, with his inimitable
sense of humor.

At first, my father used a cane. Now, he uses a walker.
A wheelchair is tucked into the corner of the closet in the
den. He's already thinking ahead to what may be. When
I see him struggle, I take a deep breath, watch, and wait,
slowly accepting what is happening to him. There is nothing for me to do but to be present with him. He will ask
for my help when he needs it. I follow my mother's lead
to let my father do as much for himself as he still can—to
dress himself, put himself to bed, and use the computer.

My father and I have become good friends. We understand each other in some intuitive way. I am surrendering to the physical truth that my body will not conceive or give me ease of sleep right now, and my father is surrendering to the reality that his body has developed Parkinson's. I ask my father why he isn't screaming with frustration, since he can no longer walk easily, sleep comfortably, chew properly, or even step into the shower. He tells me that self-pity is a bottomless pit. "I'm no martyr," he says.

We are each at different phases of our lives, yet we are journeying together through profound experiences that we cannot control. We let our love soften the pain.

"Sing me a song," he says.

I have always enjoyed singing with my father as he played his guitar—first as a girl, along with my siblings, and then as a married woman when I visited. Now, there is no longer the accompaniment of his guitar, but my father and I still find a way to sing together. I begin singing "Summertime," by George Gershwin, one of my father's favorites. I lead, my father's crackly voice fading in and out at certain points, surrendering to the way things are, and finding a way to embrace the moment with love.

May 25, 2003
Dear Brother René,

Thank you for reminding me that we change and at times our prayer life needs variety. For so many years, I was so full of prayer and desire to try to conceive and have children. I am so tired from the painful and long journey. Is being motherless what God wants for me? Does God want for me what I want for myself?

I read that Meister Eckhart (1260–1327), the German mystic, had said that the name of God means "birth-giver." He also stated that God is always giving birth, and we are always birthing God in us every moment of our lives. Eckhart believed that we become mothers of God, for God is always needing to be born. What do you think of that? Maybe there are many ways to give birth, just as you mentioned. I will pray to find my satisfaction in this.

Peace and God's Love,

Colette

June 10, 2003

Dear Colette,

I enjoyed your last letter. The Spirit is at work in you. I understand your questions. God is always giving birth and we do birth God. We are not God, but we are one with God. His actions are accomplished through us. All of this is real, yet it remains mysterious. It is a work of faith and trust.

You know you cannot have the desire to become a mother without it really happening. Believe it firmly and ask God to show you how you are a mother. It's possible to be a mother in the spiritual world. You can mother God in others. Your desire for motherhood pleases God and will eventually satisfy you, too. All I can say is trust, don't give up, believe in Love, and have confidence that God is at work.

With love in Him,
Brother René

In This Moment

It is night, and once again I am awake. The foghorns are
blowing, and the refrigerator is humming. I curl up on
the down-filled sofa with my pillow and a heavy blanket
and settle into the dark living room. I light a candle on the
coffee table and feel my aloneness permeate the air as the
silence in the room grows louder. There is nowhere to go.
I am in my body, and as the night moves deeper into itself,
I fall further into myself.

I can never reason with this nighttime awakening.
Sleep is the ultimate surrender, but the will cannot make
it happen. I cannot force myself to fall asleep. I am awake.
I wait. I read, pray, and listen to soft music on my iPod.

But it is not an easy surrender as the hours pass. I
pray in the words of the psalms: "Have mercy on me, O
Lord, for I am in distress. Tears have wasted my eyes, my
throat and my heart." I feel less alone as I say these words,
knowing that people have been calling out these psalms
for thousands of years. I join the lament.

Can I say, "I surrender," in this difficult moment? It
really is the only way. As I inhabit the words and repeat
them to myself, I loosen the doubt and despair packed into
this long night.

I lay the stone of distress in my palm and hold it
with love. This love lives in me. I feel it soothing me, and

I receive this gift. My tears quiet and my muscles begin to relax. I feel surrender breathe into me with its patience and compassion, deep in the cavity of my heart.

Finally, something in me can let go. I rest for a few hours. Once again, my body is teaching me the way to trust, to let go, to draw closer to God.

———————————//———————————

Seeking Surrender

Engage in the powerful practice of self-acceptance. Often, the same difficulty returns again and again, in varying degrees. "I thought I was over this," you hear yourself saying. But don't stop there. Now is the time to practice compassion toward yourself. Throughout the day, when you face a moment of tension with yourself, stop and repeat the following phrase several times: *I am choosing to be patient and understanding with myself. I am choosing to be patient and understanding with myself. I am choosing to be patient and understanding with myself.*

Over the next week, make a commitment to give yourself more self-acceptance and compassion with this simple and effective practice. You can use these words, or create your own words. Write down your affirmation on a piece of paper, and carry it around with you as a gentle reminder.

———————————//———————————

Breaking Through

One afternoon, while I am standing in the cereal aisle at the grocery store, I run into a woman from yoga class shopping with her two children after school. We exchange a greeting, and she introduces me to her five-year-old son and eight-year-old daughter, both wearing navy-blue-and-white school uniforms. I know from small talk before class that she is a busy mother.

I finish my shopping, and as I am leaving the store, I notice a sinking feeling in my chest. *I will never be that woman*, I think to myself.

But as I am getting into my car in the parking lot, I catch the murmur of a new voice emerging. *Let me love my life and trust its path*, I think to myself. Can I pay attention to these words? I put the keys in the ignition, but I don't start the car just yet. This is the voice of surrender breaking through, urging me to let go and inviting me in—if only I am willing to listen. *Let me love my life and trust its path*, I repeat to myself.

It is in the small moments, such as at the grocery store, or the park, or a family gathering, where I hear the words of surrender breaking through. But I don't always listen. Sometimes I do. Sometimes I don't. I notice that paying attention to sensations in my body—a rush of tears, an unsettled stomach, a strain in my voice, or a thickness in my chest—is a doorway into what is stirring within me. The body speaks, and it helps me stop and listen.

As I drive home with the ingredients for tonight's dinner in my canvas shopping bag, I think about the joy of making fresh salmon, jasmine rice, and asparagus for dinner and sharing it at the dining-room table with my husband. I let this moment become full and feel it softening my heavy heart.

The next time I am in the cereal aisle at the grocery store, I decide to pick up a box of something that I've never tried before, knowing that with awareness and grace I can make a new choice.

July 7, 2003

Dear Brother René,

Thank you for writing. It really lifts my spirits to hear from you. Although I am doing better, I now feel myself called to surrender even more. It's not as though one surrenders once and that's the end of it. It is a daily occurrence, deepening over time. It's a strange feeling because what I had thought about my life is changing.

I see now that what we want is only what we want, but what God wants for us is really the deeper truth. It feels really humbling. Have you ever struggled with surrender or has it come easily for you? How have you experienced surrender?

Peace and God's Love,

Colette

July 21, 2003

Dear Colette,

So much of the spiritual life is caught in this one word—surrender. You ask what has surrender meant in my life? Well, the prayers that are most important to me are all prayers of surrender: "Thy will be done," "Into Your hands," "Use me as You will."

By nature or the grace of God, I do not find surrender hard when relating to God and to faith. But when it comes to certain things, then I can know resistance and a hardening of attitude, just like anyone else. I pray for the grace to know God's will and the grace to do it. In our surrender we still carry on life every day as usual. One must not lose one's ego-self as we direct our steps each day.

In your first paragraph you end by saying "It feels really humbling." When one stands before God, before the power of Creation, there can be no better expression of love than this statement. Nor any greater word of praise and gratitude either. How blessed you are to have expressed your love with these words.

How blind and small one would be to say or feel (when one is conscious of the presence of God), "How great I am." God wants us to feel good in His presence (very good) to be sure, but that is because of the power of his love for us. All God's work is love because God is love.

With Love in Him,
Brother René

Finding Inspiration

It is summer, and I am in a colonial town in Mexico on a two-week vacation with my husband. A good friend is lending us her house here. She is a painter who loves the vibrancy of color in Mexico. The concrete floors are painted deep blue, and the walls are painted dusty pink and ochre. This is an unfamiliar landscape, where we do not speak the language nor understand the customs. We eat papaya sprinkled with lime juice for breakfast and fresh corn tortillas for lunch. This unknown place is a mirror of how I am feeling in my life—uncertain, watchful, and curious about meeting the unexpected.

As I walk around the town, I notice mosaics all around me, formed out of colorful ceramic tiles, some depicting the Virgin of Guadalupe, others portraying plants, palm trees, birds, bowls of fruits, or fountains. The designs are on display in restaurants, churches, parks, and courtyards. They fill me with inspiration, holding the promise that something new can be created out of fragmented pieces.

My husband and I settle into the house. There is a rooftop garden, overflowing with red bougainvillea and laundry lines for drying our clothes in the afternoon sun. Since the house is spacious, we each find a space of our own, where we can lay out our notebooks, laptops, and reading materials. I am also here to paint, so I put out my art supplies, paper, watercolors, and a variety of pencils.

I sit alone in the small studio near the garden and feel a passionate urge to create pulsing in my veins. I begin to paint a series of crosses, images I have never worked with before. I surrender to the discovery that happens in the creative process, when goals are set free so the imagination can soar. My husband sits at a long wooden table in the living room and works on writing short stories, surprising himself with an attraction to fiction, when for years he exclusively wrote poetry.

I begin to see that something new is being generated from our broken dreams. Together, my husband and I are making our own mosaic from our experiences: first the years as a young couple dreaming about having a family, then the years of wanting children, and now the present without them. Each fragment of time, piece by piece, creates a pattern of desire, loss, surrender, and love.

There is no blueprint to follow. No one can do this surrendering for me. I am placing one tile after another, using the pieces to create something new.

Seeking Surrender

Ask yourself: *Is there something new I would like to create in my life?* In your journal, respond to the question. Let yourself hear your desires by filling up the page with words, phrases, and drawings. Give yourself complete freedom to write anything that comes to mind. Sometimes writing quickly is helpful. For example, you could write, slow down on Saturdays, read more, create a prayer space at home, or be more content—anything that your heart is yearning for. When you are done, pause for a moment, and reflect on what you've written. What feels the most important to you right now? Listen to your deepest self. Then, take one of your responses, and make a list of specific ways you could fulfill your desire. Be sure to include concrete actions you can take to manifest something you would like to create in your life.

In the Heart

I have often sensed that the purpose of my life is to love. I met my husband in college when I was nineteen and living away from home in a school dorm. For most of my childhood my mother struggled with alcoholism, while my father chased after a successful career as a neurosurgeon. There was the constant undertone of loneliness in our house.

The difficult years from my childhood etched deep scars in my heart, as they do for many of us, carrying the potential to destroy our spirits. As a teenager, I longed for a true companion, and when I first met the man who would eventually become my husband, my longing to love opened up freely and unrehearsed. This impulse, bursting forth without hesitation, gave me a trust in the power of unequivocal desire.

My husband and I met at a café in Montreal, Canada. I was attending the University of New Hampshire and happened to be visiting the city with a group of friends.

While waiting in line at the coat check, I asked the person in front of me if he knew a good place to go dancing nearby. He didn't, but a voice behind me said, "Try *L'Oxygen* down the street."

I turned around, and there he was, the man that would one day become my husband. He was slim with a headful of curly brown hair, and he had a boyish look in his jean jacket. Our eyes comfortably met. I asked him to join our group, and as we sat together at a large round table, with the sounds of voices and music around us, we immediately felt at home with each other. Perhaps too young to settle down and both of different nationalities, we went our separate ways after college.

But five years later, as destiny would have it, we ended up reconnecting. I was in my mid-twenties, and living with a friend in an apartment in San Francisco, applying to graduate schools. One evening, while sitting at my desk in my drafty bedroom, huddled near the space heater, I decided to update my address book. When I came across his number, I impulsively picked up the phone and dialed. We talked for more than an hour, feeling as comfortable and at home with each other as we always had. We stayed in touch, decided to see each other again, and eventually got married.

Now, after many years, I have learned that surrendering to the daily needs of marriage takes patience, faith, and constant commitment. Just as Brother René's life is rooted in both commitments to God and to a community that supports his spiritual journey, marriage is rooted in the mingling of self and other.

As I turn toward acceptance, I reconnect with my impulse to love. It is time for me to extend beyond my loss, to stop defining my life by it. In the heart of surrender, there is an urgent life force wanting to push out and express itself. It is love. I allow for this alchemy to occur, for transformation to happen, in subtle and simple ways.

One evening, while my husband and I are cleaning up after dinner, I begin to say, "If only we would have . . ." I catch myself and let the words evaporate,

"What did you say?" he asks, over the running water as he washes the dishes.

I pause. "That was a great a dinner. Thanks for cooking," I say.

"Sure thing," he says with a smile.

August 1, 2003

Dear Brother René,

Your reminder that God is love was so important for me to hear. No matter what happens in my life, I am created from love, sustained by love and nurtured by love. May I not forget. But, Brother René, it is still difficult for me. Every day I look around and I see that I am different from other women, and I need so much faith to trust in my path. Surrender is hard for me at times, I must admit.

Warmly,

Colette

August 11, 2003

Dear Colette,

I am aware that God is working in you and that His only possible mode of action is Love. Therefore I know you try hard to surrender, and God asks no more than this from us.

You said you look around and you seem to be different than other women. No, the real truth is we are all, every one of us, different from everyone else. Yet, I know what you mean. So I suggest you try to look at yourself through God's eyes.

How does God look at you? Maybe Mark can help you to answer this question. See how he looks at you, and if it is through eyes of love (which we know it will be), then realize that since God is love, he is thus looking at you through God's eyes.

It dawns on me too that one can surrender to God because God is love. Well, I have reflected on your letter and will send it off with Love!

United in Prayer,

Brother René

Everything in Love

My father would like a warm robe to wear in his drafty house during the winter months. My mother keeps the heater on, but it's not enough with my father's frail, thinning body. He asks me to find him something in San Francisco. Since he enjoys wearing the black cashmere sweater

I bought him a few years ago, he has decided to entrust me with this new request. I can count the times on one hand that he has asked me to do anything for him, so I willingly oblige, and in a way I am honored.

I know it's also a way of helping out my mother with caring for him, since she is busy with grocery shopping, preparing meals, running errands, and bringing him the Eucharist from church, which he looks forward to receiving. So, I will shop and bring the robe with me on my next visit during my Christmas break.

At Nordstrom, I find a navy-blue fleece robe that I think will be perfect. My father looks good in blue with his olive skin tone and snowy white hair. I pack the robe snugly in a large shopping bag, ready to carry it on the flight. I place the receipt in a kitchen drawer, since my father is very particular about clothes, and if he does not absolutely like something, he will not keep it—a trait that I also possess.

When the day of my departure arrives, I am tired from the accumulation of a period of difficult and fractured sleep. It takes tremendous effort for me to pack, get the shuttle to the airport, pull my bags through security, and finally make it onto the crowded plane during this busy season.

I end up storing the large shopping bag under my seat, hearing it crunching underneath me during the flight. But it's a short trip from San Francisco to Palm Springs.

When my father puts on the robe, he instantly likes it. It fits him, hanging perfectly on his round shoulders and falling just below his knees. For years afterward, he wears the robe draped over his clothes, shielding his frail body. He feels at home in it day and night.

There isn't much left in my father's closet now—a handful of white T-shirts, a few pairs of pants and sets of pajamas, several shirts and sweaters, and a plaid cap and wool beret. The navy-blue fleece robe hangs prominently in the center of his closet. "It's special to me," he tells me many times.

Seeking Surrender

The Benedictine monks have a motto: Do everything with love. Try living this motto today by paying attention to where and how you can bring more love forward—through words of encouragement, by offering to help someone, or by listening without judgment to another person. Notice that even the slightest intention to bring love into your day changes the tone of your actions. Even something as simple as packing lunch for yourself and your family can be done with a heart of love, as you prepare a sandwich, rinse an apple, and add a little treat in the bag.

Inside Trust

Over the years, since my sister's death, my father has watched me struggle with insomnia. During many visits, I cry in the morning in front of him, over my morning tea and his cup of coffee. My father encourages me to be patient with what I'm going through. He believes in blessings in disguise, and he has told me many times, "God writes straight with crooked lines."

My father gives me his copy of the book *Abandonment to Divine Providence*, written in the eighteenth century by Jean-Pierre de Caussade, a French Jesuit priest. It is a small book of 120 pages, in which my father has underlined and annotated many passages with red pen marks in the narrow margins. I want to listen to what he has listened to. One of his underlined passages stands out: "Everything can lead to a union with God."

Before I had ever encountered any difficulty sleeping, I thought that I was always in control of sleep. I slept on my own terms and was only awake at night when I wanted to be, whether I was staying out late with friends or traveling on an evening flight. But now, the inability to sleep arrives on its own terms, and what I thought I had control over is not necessarily the case.

Over the years, I have tried many approaches to handling insomnia. I have found different ways to respond, sometimes with success, and other times with difficulty. Yet, I notice the more I can let myself be held by love when I am awake, the more I can stay calm.

This is a new orientation for me: to be held and not to be holding. Once I bring acceptance to myself in the moment, I am able to release the gripping and fear. Then I can take in the very substance of love enveloping me, comforting me, and holding me. I feel such sweetness there, in a love pouring into me like a fountain.

Here I am, trusting and receiving what is being offered to me. My body absorbs this gift, my muscles and skin release into the soft cotton sheets, and I find rest.

September 7, 2003
Dear Brother René,

I am going through more layers of grief. It is one thing to say I surrender, but another to actually live it. To live surrender is a daily act of faith. Sometimes, I wonder how God is working in my life, and at times I feel totally confused. Is God speaking to me through my life?

I am just so vulnerable right now, stripping away my desires, and feeling an emptiness. I trust that this process will allow new things to grow in me, but it's painful, and at moments I am in distress and feel sorrow piercing my heart.

I have read your last letter many times, and I find it consoling to look at myself through God's eyes. When I do, I feel more peaceful. I feel a very comforting and complete kind of love. This is a deep and powerful meditation. Thank you. I see what you mean by surrender being rooted in God's love. It turns surrender into an act of receiving love.

In spiritual friendship,
Colette

September 26, 2003
Dear Colette,

It is a blessing that you are now coming to grips with your feelings and pain. I trust you are discussing everything with Mark. We must always have confidence that God is at work in our lives, even if we are at a loss to understand what is happening. When periods of darkness pass, you will be stronger, and peace will surely return.

God will not fail you. God cannot fail you. He is Love. Because of this truth, we must change our understanding of whatever happens in our life. It is this positive outlook that is the fruit of faith. Ask God for deeper faith. So always be positive, look for the best, expect the best, and be confident.

God is saying something to us through our lives. I can't say what He is saying to you, because He is only speaking to you. You need to listen and really ask God to open your ears and heart to hear. God does only ask and want a personal relationship with you—nothing more.

Fall is here in Kentucky. The color is wonderful. Our Brother Giles died a wonderful death two days ago. We had the funeral this afternoon. He is at peace after sixty-two years as a monk. Age ninety-three.
United in Prayer,
Brother René

Pouring Out

It is a rainy weekend in early fall, and my husband and I are at the beautiful Santa Sabina Retreat Center in northern California. We gather around the stone fireplace with twenty other people to share in this seasonal retreat, watching the crackling fire burn for hours. A Camaldolese Benedictine monk, who has lived many years in New Guinea, leads us. "There, the fire is the life of the community," he tells us.

So, the fireplace becomes the center of our retreat. In the mornings and the evenings, we gather around the hearth, as the spirited and passionate monk guides us in various reflections and meditations. He invites us to enter the transformative nature contained in the elements of the burning fire: the wood, light, smoke, and ash.

We find release in the intense heat of the flames, penetrating us until we have to peel off our wool sweaters. I am pouring out the consuming grief that has been living in me for so long—with sweat, tears, and long moments of silence staring into the flickering flames. As the piles of wood keep burning, I am unloading all that has built up in me over the years.

One evening, our retreat leader asks us to jot down on a slip of paper something that is separating us from a deeper connection to our lives and ourselves—and ultimately to God and the creative spirit of life. I scribble the words: "I am carrying a feeling of failure inside myself." The resounding word *failure* stares at me: its weight, its gravity. I know I must let this go, this secret that is burning a hole right through my heart.

Then, in a ceremonial gesture, the monk invites us to throw the scraps of paper into the fire to burn and become ashes. I am mesmerized by this communal offering, each person surrendering and pouring out the burdens of the past. Everyone has something to burn, something for the blazing fire to transform.

I pray now: *Dear God, I feel your fire in me, but so much has been suffocating it. I want to trust my life, no matter what is happening. Let your fire burn in me, release me, heal me, and free me.*

Between my reflections, I gaze at my husband, watching the amber light glowing on his warm cheeks. Together, we draw on the power of the fire to transform us and clear the way for new growth to thrive.

Seeking Surrender

You can learn to let go, in big and small ways. First, be willing to notice when and how you hold on to things for too long—such as a difficult conversation, a feeling of anger toward someone, or self-criticism. Remember that noticing is a practice and is helpful in gaining self-awareness.

Next, you can utilize the method of establishing a "Let Go" box. Here's a way to create one and engage in the practice:

1. Get the following supplies: a small box with a lid, a pad of paper, and a pen.
2. Keep all your materials in a designated place—on your bedside table, at your desk, or even in your dresser drawer.

3. On a daily basis, write down whatever you find yourself
   holding on to.
4. Put the pieces of paper into the "Let Go" box, and
   remember that once you put them in the box, you have
   decided to let these things go.
5. When the box fills up, without rereading them, you can
   ceremoniously burn the pieces of paper or simply throw
   them away.

Try this method for at least one month to begin to see
the benefits—and there are many.

———————————— // ————————————

Filled with Love

"Papa, let me cut your nails for you," I say. Once a skilled
neurosurgeon capable of handling delicate instruments in
his thick and dexterous hands, my eighty-four-year-old
father can no longer clip his own fingernails. I watch him
surrender over the years to the deterioration and weak-
ening of his body. He eats less, talks less, and rests more.

At first, my father is reluctant to have me cut his nails.
He was always the one in control, but now he needs my
help. He must surrender to receiving care from others. It is
our ritual when my husband and I come to visit. I clip his
nails, and my husband trims his hair. We sit at the dining
table, and I lay out the file, the nail clippers, and the nail-
brush. I prepare a warm bowl of soapy water to soak his
fingers in. He watches me intently.

I am always a little nervous when I first begin, afraid I may cut him or not please him enough, but as I let go into the experience, the moments fill with love. I take my time, sometimes up to a full hour, filing each nail carefully, going back and forth as my father checks the corners of each nail for any remaining sharpness. "How's that Papa? Feel better?" I ask. "You always do such a good job," he says, smiling.

Over time, my father receives more care. My husband becomes his "barber from San Francisco," as he likes to call him, and every time we visit, my husband gives him a shave and a haircut. My father is always delighted to look in the mirror afterward, and for a moment, he recognizes himself again.

Surrender allows my father to receive more freely. He allows us to give more lovingly, more compassionately, and to be less afraid of what is slipping away.

October 23, 2003

Dear Brother René,

Thank you for writing. I often share your letters with Mark. We both like your advice to look for the best in life. He is still struggling to find a good work situation. I pray he finds a path that will bring him some satisfaction. He and I have such compassion for each other, and being with him is a great joy in my life.

I am becoming more aware of ways in which I am blocked from opening to the Divine—for instance, in my thinking about my life as a success or a failure. That is a very small view of life, yet all around me this is the definition that prevails. The mystery of life is so much more than this. I pray for my heart to reach this understanding. I pray to move through the barriers that prevent me from that deeper trust.

Warmly,

Colette

October 29, 2003

Dear Colette,

You do well to share your letters with Mark, as that will help him to know you even more. I will remember his intentions in prayer. I am glad my words can help you. God does bring people into our lives. His desire is for all of us to use his wisdom and love to relate to and help each other.

You speak about success and failure. Stop and put it into perspective. You are. You exist. What more could you want? Success means nothing. It is Being that counts. Think of the wonder of it all. Rejoice in the Love that brought you into existence.

Maybe instead of trying to dig deeper and understand yourself more, try looking at God. Find out who God is and what you mean when you think of your concept of God. Your concept will be very small (because God is above our thinking), but you will fill your heart with awe and wonder. All of this will be a fun activity to enjoy.

In His Love,

Brother René

P.S. In a couple of weeks, we will have a new organ set up. It will fill the church in a way we've never had before.

Through the Gate

When a novice enters the monastery, the first question he is asked is, "What do you seek?" It is the question that has been asked for centuries. Now, it is the one I am asking in my life.

As the door closes to traditional motherhood, I hear myself whispering: *What am I seeking?* Through the gate of sorrow, I have arrived at this question, longing to let go, to come to peace with my life, and to accept myself.

I share the thoughts that Thomas Merton expressed in his journals, that it is the acceptance of myself, as I truly am, that will be the doorway to transformation. I crave to meet all of myself, the deepest, unspoken self, the one who lives inside of my story. I want to more fully enter my life, in the way it is unfolding, trusting in it beyond my understanding.

I cry out to the Divine: "Let me feel your tenderness and know you are close to me." I ask for grace to come to my assistance. There is a great love burning in my heart, a love that is wide and fearless, a love that penetrates like the eyes of an owl. It is passionate, waiting for me, and able to inhabit my whole being.

What am I seeking? I place myself inside of this love, where surrender can be chiseled and carved, where I can hear the whispering of an answer: *to embrace my life and to accept myself with love.*

---------------//---------------

Seeking Surrender

Make a collage in response to the following question: What am I seeking in my life right now? Take about twenty minutes or whatever time you have. Put on some soft music, and find a place where you can be alone. You will need a piece of paper of any size, glue, scissors, and a selection of images from old calendars, magazines, or photographs.

Before you begin, be still for a few moments, allowing the question to fill your heart and your imagination. Create your collage as though you are creating a prayer. Place the images that speak to you on your paper. Image by image, listen to yourself. Be spontaneous and allow yourself to be surprised. Once you have finished, gaze at what you created and let it speak to you. Take a few minutes and write about what you created and what you discovered. Over the next week, pray with your collage. Look at it with soft, loving eyes, and ask God to help you see what is being revealed to you.

---------------//---------------

A Place of My Own

I decide to create a space in my house where I can retreat and reconnect to myself, a place for solitude, prayer, and creativity. I imagine it to be both a hermitage and a studio. My husband helps me draw up the plans but says repeatedly, "Make it the way you like."

On a modest budget, we hire a carpenter to build an inexpensive and simple twelve-by-ten-foot structure in the corner of our backyard, tucked beneath a large magnolia tree. It is one large room, with high ceilings, a slanted roof with skylights, a square window near the front door, and a small sink.

I put a cloth-covered rocking chair in one corner, a table with my art supplies in another corner, and a metal-framed image of the Virgin of Guadalupe in the alcove near the door. I am inspired by the notion of the monk's hermitage, a space that fosters solitude and contemplation for insight and awareness to emerge. I am also inspired by the artist's studio, a place to explore and create. The creamy white walls are left bare, so I can pin my canvases and sheets of paper on them.

Today, I pull out a large piece of thick white paper and pin it up to the wall. I take a black piece of charcoal and begin drawing in thin lines on the smooth surface. There is a bird on the edge of the shore, alone. His wing is broken. He cannot fly, and the winter winds have begun. The tears begin. These are the forgotten dreams of the bird that cannot fly. I begin to draw tiny dots—dots of sadness. I cannot do anything at this moment but draw tiny dots of sadness. There are no more thoughts to think about all that has happened. I draw a large bowl at the bottom of the paper. This bowl is for my tiny dots of sadness when they fall.

The motion of the charcoal on the paper is soothing. The physical sensation gives me release. I follow the soft line across the page. I hear it whispering to me, reassuring me, holding me, holding God near me. I close my eyes and lean in very close to the piece of paper. The lines are breathing across the paper. Little bird, you will fly again one day.

It feels good to be alone in here—to absorb the silence, to be with my own company, and to pray and paint. As I sink into myself, I sense something new yet undiscovered is alive underneath the sadness and disappointment. Something wants to be uncovered and brought into the light. I watch as the first new buds begin to open on the Magnolia tree outside the window.

December 3, 2003

Dear Brother René,

I wish I could feel completely confident in my life and be able to fully surrender my desires to God. I have moments, but they come and go. I find consolation in the words by the mystic Dag Hammarskjold, as he said, "Night is drawing nigh. How long the road is. But, for all the time the journey has already taken, how you have needed every second of it."

These days all I can trust is that love is what life is all about. I pray to really live from love, to be the light of divine love in my actions, words, and thoughts. As you have told me many times, God's love will fulfill me.

Enclosed please find our Christmas gift and wishes
to you. How is the new organ?
In His Love,
Colette

December 27, 2003
Dear Colette,
Peace. Joy. Love.

Thank you for your card and the warm socks. I will
use them well. Blessed New Year to you and Mark. All
I can truly say is that only God knows what the deepest
meaning of your desire really is, even if you do not. It is
not a question of simply being passive while God does
all the rest. Ask for His desire to be revealed to you. We
actually work together with God in creating

To be filled with Love is one thing, but it must always
be given away continually. The more you give, the more
you get. Never let the ball stop with you. Make an effort
to give love and to give love and to give love. Stop giving,
and it turns sour. Remember: it's not feelings that count
as much as actions.

The new organ is very fine and also very big.
United in Prayer,
In His Love,
Brother René

Listening

I continue to meet with my spiritual director. The process of letting go and of acceptance is ultimately a spiritual one for me. I feel comfortable in this quiet, intimate room on the lower level of her house. We sit across from one another, in soft upholstered chairs. There is a round table in the corner of the room, with a glass vase that is always filled with seasonal flowers—white lilies in the spring and yellow roses in the summer.

I find so much freedom here. I can talk, cry, laugh, or be silent. In the process, I am discovering God more and more—in my relationships, my marriage, my sleeplessness, my creative desires, as well as my daily work. Everything is connected to the Spirit. I also talk about my spiritual companionship with Brother René. I share the insights I am gathering from our correspondence, the inspiration I find from his confidence in God, and the power of love.

My spiritual director has read the published journals of Thomas Merton and has great appreciation for the monastic way of life. She, too, finds encouragement in the daily faithfulness of the monk's life: to pray, to work, to be silent, to be obedient, and to offer hospitality.

Each time I visit, I lean into the soft chair and share my journey. At times, I feel intense darkness and doubt, as I grapple with loss, fear, and confusion, while at other moments, I touch a sense of peace and trust that unburdens my heart and frees my spirit. In this room, I have met myself, and I have met my real life: all that had and had not happened, and the absolute emptiness I have felt. There is an element of honesty in spiritual direction that allows for new growth. I am beginning to see my life as so much more than pursuing only what I wanted or expected. As my spiritual director reminds me, "There are different paths for the same desire."

Ultimately, I find the process healing, and I begin to feel drawn toward becoming a spiritual director. As I share this idea with friends and family, it starts to crystallize, leading me to apply to a local training program. This is a transition time for me. I find myself standing in a revolving door, at the axis point where entering and exiting are lined up. I am letting go of one version of my life and stepping into the unwritten pages.

Seeking Surrender

Notice when fear arrives at your door. The willingness to recognize fear and then consciously make a choice away from it is a powerful action. Be willing to acknowledge your fear by saying, "Fear, I know you are here right now, but you are not the truth." The best antidote to fear is to turn in the direction of faith by doing something life affirming: take a walk, give someone a hug, cook a good meal, sing a song, or engage in some form of prayer. Creative actions can move you away from fear and into the power of love unfolding in the present moment.

———————————— // ————————————

Honoring the Path

My husband and I have been looking into adoption on and off for several years. After attending seminars, talking with people, and many hours of soul-searching, we have decided it is not the right path for us. Our decision is disconcerting at first, even shocking to us, but after all we have been through we need to trust our intuition and judgment. Thoughts haunt me: I will have no descendants, I will never be called Mama, and I will be alone when I am old. *Can I live without what I had wanted for so many years? Can I allow a life that looks so different from others—and so different from what I had hoped for and expected?*

I have always known myself in comparison to others, from being raised in a family of ten children and regarding myself as number eight. But now the journey of surrender calls for me to see myself as a uniquely created being with my own destiny and path. This insistence to measure my life against others has been a burden, and I can no longer walk in my life carrying around this weight.

"Do you have children?" someone at work will ask me.

"No, my husband and I were unable to have children, and we decided not to adopt," I answer.

At first, the words sound heavy and perhaps defensive. Still, I feel I must say them. I need to fit my story into the world, along with the mothers, grandmothers, and single women. It is time for me to take my place. Speaking my truth is an act of surrender.

I call the adoption agency and request to have our file removed from circulation. We have decided to let go, and with that release comes a softness curling around the edges of my heart. Acceptance is a welcome relief, even as I grapple with settling into my truth. *God, I trust you with my life*, I say, again and again, until it becomes a daily mantra.

February 27, 2004
Dear Brother René,

Trust all is well, and uniting our prayers during this Lenten season. This has been a time of deep reflection, and after honest discernment and listening to the wisdom in our hearts, Mark and I have decided not to pursue any more options for having children. We have decided to let go. This feels sad, surely, and there is some doubt lingering, but we are trusting that this is the right path for us.

What a momentous decision! One I will never understand fully. This is surrender beyond what I can even comprehend. May the grace of divine love hold us firmly in trust, hope, and faith.

Thank you for all your love and support for us. Now my life feels a little strange to me, somewhat unfamiliar, even confusing. It is not the life I was planning to have. I also wanted to share the good news that Mark got a job in the communications department of a state government

agency. I hope his new position works out for him. Thank
you for your prayers.

Peace, always. In God's love,

Colette

March 4, 2004

Dear Colette,

Thank you for your letter. You did well in your decision. You surrendered it all to God with your *fiat* (Let it
be done). It was no small decision. You surrendered to
the King of the Universe, to the all-powerful God, the
all-knowing God, the all-loving God, to the Creator who
said, "Let it be!" and all of creation existed.

Yet remember to think of such an act (of surrendering one's desires) as being positive. You surrendered to
Love. Have no fears or doubts.

Glad to hear the good news about Mark's job.

With Love,

Brother René

Clearing the Way

For many years, my husband and I have used the second bedroom in our house as an office, waiting to fill it
with furniture and things for a child. Year after year, it has
remained in an in-between state, with an unstained pine
desk, a sofa bed that needs a new mattress, and a jam-
packed filing cabinet.

Finally, with the recognition that there will be no business or child to fill the room, we begin to empty out the wanting and waiting that have accumulated within these walls. We recycle the unnecessary paperwork stuffed into file folders, fill boxes with useless binders of information and old notebooks, and clear out our past dreams.

There is another path to follow, a way to live without constant conditions.

While sorting through things, I find a slip of paper with a quote by Thomas Merton I had written down while visiting Gethsemani, in which he is summarizing Romano Guardini. He writes, "The will of God is not a fate to which we submit, but a creative act in our life producing something absolutely new."[2]

As my husband and I clear out the space, fill the recycling container, and take our boxes and bags to the donation bin of Goodwill, it's as if we are preparing for something—not what we had planned for but, rather, something new and different than what we were expecting.

When I reflect back to that afternoon when I first met Brother René, I think that perhaps he had been waiting for a sign to receive the topic for his jubilee talk, and somehow, I ended up delivering it to him. He wasn't expecting to meet me, and I wasn't expecting to meet him, a spiritual teacher who would influence the course of my life. Neither of us anticipated the love that would transpire between us or our precious extended correspondence.

Now, my husband and I turn toward the unexpected. We leave a door inside ourselves slightly ajar, so the unknown, the mystery, the way of God, can enter. We paint the walls in the second bedroom a moss green color, and we get a new bookcase, armchair, and daybed with throw pillows. The room becomes a cozy place to read and relax. We spread out and begin to live in the entire house. There is more space to occupy.

———————————*//*———————————

Seeking Surrender

Reflect on what needs to be cleared out in your house—both your interior and exterior house. Start this reflection by placing your hands on your lap with your palms up in a gesture of surrender. Remain in this posture as you take a few deeper breaths, allowing yourself to relax and become receptive. Feel yourself opening like a flower in the warmth of the morning sun.

Next, slowly and meditatively, ask yourself: *What needs to be cleared out in my life?* Repeat the question, and sit with it for as long as necessary, until the response feels like it's from your heart. The answer may come in the form of an image or in words. Take time to write or draw your insights in your journal, and see if over the next month you can take action toward what is calling you.

———————————*//*———————————

Grace

I am dancing with my husband in the living room on a Friday night. We have just finished our dinner of roast chicken with yams and French string beans. We move slowly in a circle in front of the crackle and warmth of our fireplace. I love this man. He is in my arms. I don't know where I'm going right now, but I open myself to love. We cannot do this alone. There is a strange emptiness in the air when the music ends, but we keep dancing in the silence.

April 2, 2004
Dear Brother René,

Thank you for your letter. You are always so positive and uplifting when you write. You are also so solid in trusting God and believing strongly in Love. Your words are good for me to hear. For me, I experience God's love in a very personal and tender way. The other day, I sensed God saying: "Give your desire to Me." What more is there really to say?

I am in a quiet time right now as Mark and I settle into our decision. I pray for God to fill me more and more with love. I am sending you a recommendation form for a spiritual direction program I am hoping to attend. I am discerning where God is calling me now, and perhaps spiritual direction is a path for me. I want to live from the heart.

Peace,
Colette

April 22, 2004

Dear Colette,

Your listening qualities are very good—hearing the calling to give your desires to God.

And being Love, God can only answer you with Love to your ultimate joy. All God asks and what He dearly wants is our desire. Desire is God's voice speaking in our hearts. It is a gift to us. It is a longing of the heart for its fulfillment. You know, you cannot long for something that is not there. By that I mean you must have God already in your heart in order to have a desire for God.

Always remember that you surrendered to the One who loves you, with an infinite love, full of Fire. How could you not trust such a one? Don't hesitate. Don't feel alone.

Yes, I did answer the questions on the spiritual direction reference. Hope you are able to attend.

United in Prayer,

In His Love,

Brother René

A Close Look

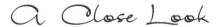

I make a yearly pilgrimage to see the wildflowers at a particular spot on the Northern California coast. Here, hundreds of flowers grow on the hillside called Chimney Rock, a rugged bluff fully exposed to the windy weather. Wearing windbreakers, scarves, and knitted caps, my husband and I follow a dirt trail out to see these resilient little flowers—red Indian paintbrush, baby blue eyes, yellow buttercups, California poppies, white irises, and purple lupines.

I bend down low to take a close look at a tiny buttercup, amazed at how this small flower can withstand such strong wind. The trembling petals are held firmly by its stem, with strong roots in the earth. For me, this is a holy experience, to admire the beauty that grows on its own accord, year after year, despite the demanding conditions.

Hundreds of people make this journey every year, and as we pass one another on the path along the way, we share a moment of recognition that we are seekers. We nod. We smile. We say hello. We find inspiration and even courage in these wild flowers that sit on the hillside yielding to the forces of nature in complete surrender.

Seeking Surrender

Practice a form of walking prayer. Find a place where you can observe nature and slowly walk for twenty minutes or more. As you are walking, look at the sky, the trees, the plants, the wind, the mountains, or the water. All around you in the natural world, you can see the organic movement of surrender: a tree surrendered in the wind, a plant surrendered in the sunlight, a bird surrendered in flight. Reflect on what season it is, observe whether the plants are in bloom or dormant, notice the weather, and observe the daily continuum of the sky moving from day to night. Let nature teach you about surrender.

———————— // ————————

On Strong Wings

The morning light fills the kitchen, and breakfast is placed upon the table once again. I look older now. My husband looks older now. Strands of gray hair run through our brown hair. More thin lines curl around the corners of our eyes. There's a tenderness in aging together, as we stand hand-in-hand in the cathedral of time. We enter another period in our married life, bringing forward the scars from loss and the resilience from love.

I remember the friction during our first year of marriage. My husband and I were both strong willed and needed to learn how to live together. We had to blend our individual preferences and find a union, as we started making decisions about everything and anything, from what we ate for dinner, to how we spent our money, to what we did during our summer vacation. It was a delicate balance between self and other. Sometimes we felt compromised, and sometimes we felt understood. In that give and take, there was the constant interplay of surrender and resistance.

After journeying through my many years of marriage, I have come to understand that there are days when the commitment, not the feeling, carries us through. There is the need for gentle obedience. Over the years, we have made many decisions together, with various outcomes.

Some choices have given us satisfaction, while other ones have brought us discontent.

Soon after my husband closed his small business and took a full-time job, I came home one evening from having dinner with a friend and found him sitting at the dining-room table, staring into the computer screen. The lights were off, and when I asked him what he was doing, he muttered this and that.

I took his hand and led him to the sofa. Together we curled up, and I wrapped a chenille blanket around us. We sat with the lights off for a long time. "Nothing has worked out," he said, choking up. "It's okay," I said softly. "It's okay," I repeated the words.

In the silence, I remembered what my father once told me about the value of disappointments: "They make you humble," he said, "and humility can give you the gift of looking at things in a new way."

As we live with certain unfulfilled dreams and expectations, we hold on to the promise of love and do not let it erode. We surrender to the truth that life is not at our command. Time and experiences have changed us into who we are in this moment, giving us the gift of seeing things another way. We are allowing the grace of our lives to shape us. In the new day, my husband and I are both a little older, a little stiffer, and a little more in love.

May 27, 2004
Dear Brother René,

I am changing. I feel myself going deeper into God. And I am expanding. God is more than if I had a child or not. This is a big trust—a release into God's fullness. Speak to me about humility.

I built a small studio in my backyard that I use for writing and painting, and also have the desire to use it as a hermitage.

Warmly,

Colette

June 8, 2004

Dear Colette,

Thank you for your letter. I liked very much when you said, "God is more than if I had a child or not." That is so so so true. Yet God is bending over backwards looking for our attention so as to express His love for us. God gave us the desire to be loved and to seek God. But it has to be a free gift from ourselves to God. That is humility.

What determines a hermitage is the aloneness with the alone. With your mind and desire on God, you are alone with God. You are not looking at yourself to see what image you project to others. I wish you well on your adventure.

With Love,

In Him,

Brother René

Unfolding Light

The morning fog begins to burn off, and the sun shines through the square windows in my studio. I write in my notebook: "I don't know my path at this moment, and in this small studio, which is my hermitage, it is so delightful not to know. It is so peaceful not to worry about it and to live life as it unfolds."

These days when I look in the mirror, I don't quite know what I am seeing. There are contradictions: the desire for fullness and the desire for nothing; the desire to know and the truth of not knowing; the need for stillness and the urge to produce.

I have no big goals. My only plan is to be in this dwelling, in this private space, alone and uninterrupted, for as long as time permits. Here, I pour out my longing and uncertainty into the paintings I make, the words I scribble, and the incense and prayers I offer.

There is a tradition to a hermitage, to a sacred space for solitude, where every breath, every word, and every stroke of a paintbrush is received—belonging completely to the self, yet experienced beyond the self. Thomas Merton had a hermitage. Saint Francis of Assisi had a hermitage. Virginia Woolf had a room of her own.

I follow the tradition of the seeker who goes into the desert, a cave, a tent, an art studio, or a one-room dwelling to "be alone with the alone," as Brother René would put it. The intention is to encounter solitude, discovering what the silence wants to bring forth.

Here, in this room, I am reminded of Brother René's teachings. I surrender to God, to love, to creation. I lean in to the vastness of my soul and its generous capacity for compassion—a soul that is full and pulsating, always multiplying, and that is not to be measured against failure but against a greater standard, the measure of love.

In the quiet emptiness of my studio and hermitage, I offer myself to life. I am getting to know myself again, and it's a joy. I light a stick of aloe wood incense and place it upright in the sand of a small turquoise clay bowl. The sweetness lingers in the air as the smoke rises.

Outside my window, I watch the papery bamboo leaves change from light green to dark green, as the sun moves in and out of the lingering clouds. When the incense finishes burning, I resist my urge to immediately light another stick, and I take time to inhale the lingering fragrance.

Seeking Surrender

Take time to be alone so you can listen to your deepest self. You can do this at home, in nature, in a sacred space, or even in your car. Being alone allows you to get to know yourself in a special way. In the spiritual and creative journey, being alone encourages the growth of the interior life. For the next month, carve out time to be alone at least once a week.

At the beginning of the week, look at your schedule and select a thirty-minute block when you can be alone. Put it in your schedule as an appointment with yourself.

During this sacred time, be quiet. Turn the ringer off your cell phone, and do not check e-mail messages.

Take a walk, take a bath, draw or write in your notebook, or sit in your favorite chair and relax—decide what's right for you. It doesn't have to be the same every week. Enjoy your own company. Find a sense of solitude.

Listen to your own voice. It is saying something only you can hear.

———————————//———————————

Needle and Thread

As I look through pages of images while making a collage, I stop and gaze at a photograph in a *Smithsonian* magazine of Annie Mae, a quilter from Gee's Bend, Alabama. The woman in the photograph is now seventy-eight years old, and the image captures her pulling a threaded needle through a piece of fabric as she makes a quilt.

I absorb the moment this photograph captures— Annie Mae stitching together squares from old blue jeans and cotton shirts, thin and faded, worn by her husband and son over many years. Stitch by stitch, she pulls the thread through the fabric with her steady hand. The thread is taut but not tight, as she completes one square and starts another, creating a pattern from the details of her life.

Can I attend to my days with such steady and surrendered attention, while working, doing errands, attending to myself and others, and taking care of my home with my husband? There is an interior freedom I am seeking, in the needle and thread of time, as I am engaged in my daily actions. I make more room for the Divine to reach into the folds and creases of my being and to live in the fabric of my everyday life.

"Perhaps the Book of Life, in the end, is the book of what one has lived," Thomas Merton wrote in his journal on July 17, 1959.[3]

My body is the book of my days, containing my comings and goings, the rhythms of my nights, and all that I have loved and all that I am loving. On my soles are the imprints of miles. In my heart is stitched the tender lace of love and loss. And in the muscles of my arms, I carry the memories of all those I have held.

Within the ordinary moments that I live every day, I either open the door or close the door to surrender. As I talk, sit, eat, and sleep, the movement of surrender is living in and through me. And I am moving with it.

September 9, 2004

Dear Brother René,

My heart is yearning for a deeper connection. Sometimes when I pray I am so busy thinking about all the things in my life that I miss God altogether. Even so, I remind myself that the Spirit is always present—and I am not separate from it.

I don't want to be searching so hard and intensely that it consumes me. Sometimes, I just close my eyes, quiet the words and say: God let me know your love, live your love, and be your love. Too many ideas about God feel heavy and intrusive. So I stop pushing. I trust that God will guide me, lead me, and teach me. How do you stay content with this deep desire, within the human limitation to understand God? How do you keep your focus on God every day?

I am enjoying my hermitage. Yes, there are moments when I feel the pain of never having had a child, but I am releasing that more and more. Pray for my peace, as I pray for yours.

Warmly,

Colette

September 18, 2004

Dear Colette,

Perhaps the answer to your questions is faith. Yes, simply to believe. Remember: God is Spirit. Thus in faith you believe in God's presence. Believing in God's presence is not to be equated with feeling God's presence. We really need to be careful not to equate feeling God's presence as real and believing in God's presence as something not real. Both are truly real. Faith is actually a higher mode, so to speak, than feeling. Feelings can be deceptive.

You do well to stop pushing and to trust God will guide, lead, and teach you. Now that is an excellent act of faith. I don't keep focused on God all day long, but I do have several methods to bring me back. For instance, when seated I never cross my legs to remember I am in the presence of the Almighty, and every time I go through a door I recite a certain prayer. I also say a prayer when I bow in church. Thus when in church and someone else bows the prayer comes automatically. I find it important to use my body to help me remember God's presence.

The moments you feel the pain of not having a child of your own are simply a call to offer yourself in humble submission, trusting that this gift of trusting is pleasing to God—even going to the point of believing that not having a child will find its fulfillment in a more perfect form of motherhood for you. God leaves no one barren.

In His Love,

Brother René

Out to Sea

I watch my father physically decline. His body is a weight he carries around as he pushes a metal walker back and forth across the aqua blue living-room carpet, doing his "laps," as he calls them.

My father was always a very composed man, deliberate in his gestures and measured in his movements. As a surgeon, he learned to master his hands and body and took pride in moving with control and precision. But now, with Parkinson's, his hand trembles as he lifts a spoon to his mouth. My father has lost his familiar gracefulness, yet

I notice a deeper, ever-present grace in him, a glimmer, a light emanating from his soft brown eyes.

Over the years, I witness his aging, watching his olive skin weather and become dry, hearing his deep voice become thin, and seeing his stormy temper calm. He saw me come into this world, uttering my first cry in the open air, and now I am seeing him leaving this world, preparing for his last sigh. His aging is my aging, as we stand at the shore of this open sea, with the fierce wind blowing across our bare faces.

Far out, beyond some imaginary horizon, I see my father swimming in the sea of his soul, steadily, stroke after stroke. I ask fewer questions now, for the mystery of life and death demands my respect and silence.

December 17, 2004
Dear Brother René,

Greetings during this Advent season. How much I enjoyed your letter! I like hearing about the small ways (that become big ways) you keep God alive and keep prayer alive in your daily life. More and more I find myself saying, "I don't know." Where is God leading me right now? I don't know. Why have certain things happened? I don't know. It feels time to let the questions go and live the life that I have.

This is a time of change. Have you had times when you felt something in you changing, when you could sense that God was changing something in you, even if you couldn't put your finger on it? May the divine presence of compassion be reborn in us this season.

Warmly, in God's abundant love,

Colette

December 22, 2004

Dear Colette,

Time is catching up with me. Even my walk is much slower. Oh! Well! Now I understand what old brother Octivious meant when he said, "My body she feels like Adam, but my heart is like a teenager."

I've been quite under the weather. I can't find your letter to answer your questions. I'm doing better now. Thank you for the lovely scarf for Christmas. I'll just have to lay low for a while.

United in Prayer,

In His love,

Brother René

 Togetherness

On a clear and cool Sunday afternoon, my husband and I head to the small park near our house for a walk. It is filled with people from the neighborhood, strolling, walking their dogs, and sitting on the wooden benches. As we begin walking on the pathway through the park, I am immediately aware that my pace is quicker than my husband's today. We both notice it, and after a few minutes we end up mentioning it to each other. At that moment, we realize we have a choice—to walk separately and meet up later, or to adjust our respective paces to become more aligned and at ease. We agree to stay together.

We take a few more steps. I slow down slightly, while my husband speeds up a little. Once our pace is established, we reach out and hold hands. Over the years, we have learned that it's the daily decisions that contribute to the larger vision of our marriage. We are surrendering to a togetherness, to what it means to join one's life with another's.

We learn to walk together, again and again, in many ways. My husband and I have needed to nurture a new intimacy between us after all the years strained with the effort to conceive. We have needed to integrate this history into the present lives of our bodies. We tread lightly on the moist earth, as we begin to open, regaining faith and rebuilding what has collapsed. We move slowly, touching the tender skin that yearns for patience and delicate care. It starts with compassion.

Who can speak of love without pain? In the heart, there lives the hope that pain can be transformed. Love now becomes more generous and full. There is a story only we know, one that needs our mercy. The years have passed. This meeting of hand in hand, with less stipulations, offers us a resting place—palms together, fingers folding, familiar, warm, and giving.

As my husband and I continue to move through the many changes in our lives, surrender provides us with a new orientation, a compass of understanding and acceptance to guide us. Surrender gives us the knowledge that love holds no conditions and invites us to uncover its boundless nature. It allows us to move forward, past disappointments, preconceptions, and expectations.

Yes, today I will walk slower. It is not about compromise but about opening myself more fully to the union formed through marriage—beyond my separateness—in contact with the wind, the trees, and the one whose hand I am holding. It is about the greater love that Brother René continually refers to in his letters.

Side-by-side, my husband and I walk together. We stop to watch a pair of hawks circling above the tops of tall cypress trees. When the birds land on different branches, they call to one another in high, sharp whistles, keenly aware of each other's location.

———————————✲———————————

Seeking Surrender

Remind yourself that it doesn't need to be your way or the other's person's way—there is a third way, the way of togetherness. In the union of sharing your life with another, you live the journey of surrender. Togetherness is a path of surrender. Write a letter to yourself, recognizing all the graces you are receiving through sharing your life with others.

———————— // ————————

Into the New Day

It is silent in the house, except for the rumble of the occasional car coming down the street. I meet myself again in the middle of the night, in what I call the "in-between time," in the enigma, darkness, and stillness. I have become familiar with this moment, when I cannot descend back into the dream realm but remain on the surface of wakefulness. Even so, it is never easy for me to acquiesce, to face not being able to sleep when I want to.

"Acceptance doesn't mean you like it," a good friend tells me. "It just means you are acknowledging what is."

I hear the haunting questions linger in my mind: *What is wrong with me? Why can't I control this?* But I don't go any further. I know now it is better to stop this train of thought and to turn toward the path of acceptance, choosing to tenderly be with myself in this moment. I realize that what I can control is my response and reaction to circumstances and situations, and the way I care for myself and others.

Thomas Merton wrote in one of his journals: "For it is the unaccepted self that stands in my way and will continue to do so as long as it is unaccepted. When it is accepted, it is my own stepping stone to what is above me."[4]

I rest for a while. I have learned to rest over the years. Sometimes I drift back to sleep, and sometimes I do not. Yet, the gentleness of resting brings some ease into my body and mind, and after this, I can more lovingly face myself.

I get up and wash my face. The warm water soothes me. I head into the kitchen to make myself a cup of tea, keeping the lights dim and making as little noise as possible. I feel like a guest when I awake during the night, and I do not want to disturb its rhythm.

I sit in my bedroom chair, with candles illuminating the room, sipping my tea while writing in my notebook. In the past, I have wanted to run away and hide, but I have learned there is nowhere to go. Eventually I always end up back with myself.

I have arrived in this moment with myself once again. And the need for acceptance runs deeper than I could have ever imagined. I want to shake the night air, but surrender is asking for something else—for breathing room, for softness, and for release into the moment. There are no deals to cut with God.

Fatigue is my companion throughout this day, and rather than reject it, I adjust myself to accommodate it. If possible, I reschedule an appointment, forfeit running an errand, and pace my energy at work. I find ways to tend to myself—with a gentle swim, through a relaxing walk in the park, or by sitting quietly in a church. I give myself patience and slow down.

There is no turning back. The night passes, and the day is before me. Can I receive myself, the one who is having difficulty sleeping? There is a tired woman in me who needs my embrace and not my judgment and anger. The morning light peers through the corners of the bedroom curtain, and I enter the new day through the doorway of compassion and self-acceptance.

September 5, 2005
Dear Brother René,

I hope you are feeling well. Lately, I have been saying the prayer of Saint Ignatius of Loyola: "Take, Lord, and receive all my liberty. . . . You have given all to me. To you, Lord, I return it . . ." Do you know that prayer?

The other day I had an image that I was handing God a baby from my arms. I wasn't crying or clinging. Sometimes, though, I wonder if these images are truly from God or from my own desire. How do you discern this? I am praying for deeper and deeper healing. I feel God opening my heart wider and wider to love in a special way.

I hope you are well and enjoying the beauty of the fall season.

In God's peace,
Colette

September 13, 2005
Dear Colette,

I am feeling fine. You could hardly have a better attitude. Handing God the baby can only be understood by you. But there ought to be no doubt where it came from.

Surely it was God's action in you. It is a clear picture of your desire, and includes the willingness to present this desire into God's hands. You can do no more than this. God asks no more of you.

You wonder what could possibly give you fulfillment beyond having a child. Perhaps it is something beyond your conceiving! Something so wonderful you can't even talk about it. But it is not beyond your faith or your trust or even your desire. Is God not capable of something like that? These thoughts can even deepen your faith and hope to a greater depth. What more can I say?

I really do not know the prayer of Saint Ignatius, but the prayers I do know are along the same line—union of wills. Yes, let's keep united in prayer and in abandonment. Love is the bond and the joy and the hope.

United in Prayer,

Brother René

With Every Step

I am delighted to be accepted into the three-year spiritual direction program at Mercy Center in Burlingame, California, even if I am not entirely sure I am meant to become a spiritual director. I start attending the training sessions with a group of twenty men and women of various ages, cultural backgrounds, professions, and faith traditions. The topics we cover include identifying religious experience, the nature of spiritual direction, adult development, culture and the experiences of God, and dimensions of healing in spiritual direction.

Monthly, we come together and delve deeper into understanding the art and practice of spiritual direction. We learn that it is a way of listening *with* people, not just *to* them. Over time, we become more comfortable with talking less and listening more, trusting a deeper wisdom, as we let go of the need to have the answers. We begin to understand that each person has a unique way of relating to the Divine and what is sacred.

We are taught how to use images, words, silence, feelings, and sensations in the body as means to access, support, and encourage a person's spiritual journey. We engage in practice periods with one another, making observations and giving feedback. We also become familiar with different forms of prayer through ritual, music, sacred texts, art, meditation, and walking in nature among the two-hundred-year-old oak trees on the Mercy Center property.

In one session, we are asked to reflect on our images of and relationship with God as the foundation for understanding other people's experiences. I feel both apprehensive and curious about responding to these questions. I decide to go into the chapel, where I have prayed many times over the years while on retreats and now monthly during my training program. It is a place I can sink into myself, with privacy and comfort. I know this assignment is asking me to be honest.

I enter the chapel and can relax in the low, tranquil lighting. A simple square altar stands in the center, leaving

the front of the chapel open and empty. There I sit comfortably on the tan carpet with my legs crossed, with only
a handful of people sitting in the pews behind me.

In the silence, I ask myself, *What is my image of God?
And what is my relationship with God right now?*

As I begin to reflect, I realize that for the past decade
I have been praying for miracles, even begging at times,
to obtain what I have been longing for, to no avail. I cried
out to God while wanting and waiting to become a mother,
while my sister was slipping away, and during my long
lonely nights of sleeplessness. But instead, I have been
called to transform my understanding of what desire even
means. I have been called to let go of my preconceptions.
My image of God has become less defined, as I open to the
mystery.

Now, I have arrived in the cave of myself, no longer
tucked under the hood of my sweater, imitating the monks
as I did at the monastery, but sitting and praying to trust
that my life is holy as it is. I am in no hurry. Being in this
program is as much about personal growth and attending
to my spiritual life as it is about developing skills for a
practice.

I remember what Brother René wrote to me: "Desire is
a longing of the heart for its fulfillment." With every step,
the door opens wider. I feel at home in the spiritual direction program, following this new kind of desire, beginning
to see my life as so much more than pursuing only what I
wanted or expected. The release itself is a prayer.

---//---

Seeking Surrender

Ask yourself: *What is my image of God, of the Divine, of the Spirit?* Make a drawing, or series of drawings, to respond to the question:

1. Use crayons, pencils, charcoal, markers, color pencils, or oil pastels.
2. Use any size of paper, or draw in your journal. You can make a drawing of lines, shapes, and colors. It might not resemble any recognizable object, but it will have meaning for you. You could draw a large yellow circle that you sense is the power of God, or a black box that represents mystery to you. Allow yourself to delight in discovery and expression, without being judgmental.
3. When you are done, look with loving eyes on what emerged. Let your image speak to you. What do you see? Is there a feeling that corresponds to what you created? Take a few minutes and write about your drawing and your experience of making it.

---//---

In the Presence of Sorrow

My father wants to talk about death, not in a morbid way, but more in an honest, straightforward manner. He wants me to read him passages from the book *Journal of a Soul: The Autobiography of Pope John XXIII*. He places Post-it notes on the pages that speak of death. "Read this to me," he says, handing me the well-worn book. I take a deep breath to anchor myself. I am my father's child but no longer a child. This is my moment to be strong and sit with my father in this time of his life—in his surrendering to nature, to the passage of time, to what is beyond our control.

I hold the book, and I read to my father with an even pace, slowly and clearly. "Is this loud enough?" I ask him. "Yes, that's perfect," he says, as he leans back into his leather chair, padded with pillows and a sheepskin cushion, attempting to ease the constant discomfort in his muscles and joints. I can feel him absorbing every word I read.

> When one is nearly seventy, one cannot be sure of the future. "The years of our life are three score and ten, and even if we are strong enough to reach the age of eighty, these years are but toil and vanity; they are soon passed and we also pass away."[5]

As I read, I notice my resistance, my hesitation; but even with that, the truth of the fading light cannot be suppressed. I stay in the presence of the words, reading. How I want to hold on to my father—but I can't.

> So it is no use nursing any illusions: I must make myself familiar with the thought of the end, not with dismay which saps the will, but with confidence which preserves our enthusiasm for living, working, and serving. Some time ago I resolved to bear constantly in mind this

reverent expectation of death, this joy that ought to be my soul's last happiness when it departs from this life.[6]

An elderly friend recently reminded me that we are *of nature* and have a life cycle. Still, the sorrow at the thought of losing my father is immediate, felt deep in my bones and my heart. Yes, by nature we change, and now my father is slowly separating from this physical world. He cannot stop the change. I cannot stop the change. I will miss his warm cheek touching mine, as he hugs me and gives me a kiss in his fatherly way.

I need not become wearisome to others by speaking frequently of this; but I must always think of it, because the consideration of death, the *judicium mortis*, when it has become a familiar thought, is good and useful for the mortification of vanity and for infusing into everything a sense of moderation and calm.[7]

I share this intimate experience with my father, gripped with sorrow. This is what is deep in his being now. The words he wants and needs to hear. He is preparing for death, unsure when it will come. Loss is held in surrender. And sorrow, too. There is nothing to resist. My father would often say, "Be grateful you can feel the depth of sorrow, for that means you have really loved."

March 15, 2006
Dear Brother René,

Greetings. I have been spending more time with my aging parents. My father is eighty-four and getting more frail. I am helping my mother care for him. I see him having to let go of the things he enjoyed—certain foods, playing the guitar, swimming, reading for hours. However, he is strong in prayer, and that helps him go through the days.

My spiritual direction program is going well. They say it is a calling. I am already seeing people. Mark and I are doing well. We are so grateful to be together. Marriage for me has been a truly holy commitment, one that I continue to surrender to, open my heart to, and allow the union to transform me. I remember when we first met; you said to me that just as I had a daily companion in Mark, you had a daily companion in God.

In God's Peace,
Colette

March 21, 2006
Dear Colette,

I will put a note on the board asking the community to remember your father in prayer. What a great blessing for him to have his daughter learning spiritual direction and being there for him at this very important time in his life. Of all the people you are seeing at this present time, none can be more important for you than him. This will give you great joy and fulfillment as well as give much glory to God.

We are all just a particle smaller than an atom, but we count as a member of God's own body. Each of us is a part of God's body. Small as we are, when united we constitute God. It would be too much to try and say more.

Yes, spiritual direction is a calling, so rejoice in God's love and be grateful for this work. All will be your spiritual children. You have the desire, and this comes from God, and he will not let this desire of his in you go unfulfilled. It is you uniting your pain to God and accepting the circumstances in your life that has done this for you.
In His Love,
Brother René
P.S. Will be eighty very shortly!

Daily Living

It's a new day, but today I don't feel like stepping into it. I'm tired. My list of responsibilities is long and waiting for me. I confront my urge to lock the door and stay inside, even though the morning sun is already sending light into my bedroom window.

Sometimes, I move between resistance and surrender all day long. I just want to be somewhere else and doing something other than where I am and what I am actually doing. I notice the constricting knots in my mind and in my muscles. It is here, in this thick bramble of resistance, that I meet my need for surrender and seek its presence.

If I can bring any amount of gratitude to what is right in front of me, then some opening and release is possible. If I can enjoy the fresh blueberries at breakfast, feel the hug my husband gives me before he walks out the door to catch the bus, or hear the laughter of the children where

I work, then there is hope for light to break through the density. With each step, I can begin to surrender to what is before me.

I remember what one of the monks at Gethsemani said in a lecture he gave about his experiences in the open sea as a boy in Massachusetts. He recalled that in sailing there is the constant need to correct one's course while out in the deep water. Throughout his forty years as a monk, he found this same principle also applied to his daily spiritual commitment. He continually needed to realign himself with the profound intentions of his vows and the deepest desires in his heart.

Every day, the monks come together seven times to pray in community. Except for the 3:15 a.m. Vigils, each period begins with this prayer: *O Lord, come to my assistance. O Lord, make haste to help me.* This simple prayer recognizes the continuous need to ask for divine help in order to stay connected to the center of grace. The monks constantly seek to remember, realign, and return to the spiritual path. It is a daily action, one that is made many times throughout the course of a day.

So, I keep turning in the direction of surrender, knowing that its constant companion is resistance, and knowing that I, too, can call out: *O Lord, come to my assistance.* I am not alone.

December 17, 2006
Dear Brother René,

Mark and I send you our warmest wishes for a joyful and peaceful Christmas season. Happy Birthday for eighty! We are sending our blessings.

I am finding surrender has many dimensions and layers to it—there's always more. Living surrender is a daily journey for me, one in which I must continually ask for guidance and wisdom from the Spirit. It calls upon me to keep God at the center, as the true context of my life. Your life of surrender gives me inspiration.

Thank you for praying for my father during this time in his journey. I can tell he is at the end of his pilgrimage. He is struggling physically, and that is painful for me to witness sometimes. It's a great comfort to me to know you hold him in your prayers.

Peace and God's Love,
Colette

January 13, 2007
Dear Colette,

Thank you for your greetings. Eighty is a burden, but that's okay. One gets slower and slower, in body and mind. It takes all your time to get any place with a cane. But that is life.

I had a spot of skin cancer removed, so that's over. All else goes very well. I still work in the guesthouse and love it. I still love my life of prayer and dedication to God, and I am still searching for God who is inside of me someplace. Yes, surrender is something we live every day. It's a daily struggle. I am also aware that it pleases God very much

when we surrender. That is what he asks us to do. You
and Mark have surrendered and that gives God glory.

Trust. Hope. Surrender. Union of wills. Yes, I will
pray for your father. He too needs to surrender his life to
God—Let Go.
In His Love,
Brother René

After this letter, Brother René and I stopped our regular
correspondence. It happened quite naturally. We would
now exchange letters occasionally, and I would still send
Easter and Christmas cards, but I didn't expect to get anything back from him, and I rarely did. I believe we both
recognized that the months and years of exchanging letters
had reached its fulfillment. I also understood that he had
grown older, and his energy had changed.

Yet, I would see him one more time, several years
later, when I would make a return trip back to the abbey.

Being Together

I sit with my father in his home, and in truth we could
be anywhere, since my father doesn't go out anymore,
except for occasional doctor appointments. There are no
more restaurant outings, or walks, or visits to church or

bookstores. We sit at the kitchen table. We talk. We sit on the sofa. We talk. We sit in the den. We talk.

The talking is our way of doing something together. Most of the time, I forget half the things we say, but what lingers is the melding of our voices, the feeling of intimacy, and our desire to connect and share these moments together.

I watch my father yielding his body to Parkinson's and aging—coughing more, shaking more, the itching spreading over more of his skin. There's a long list of symptoms, and everyone experiences them differently and to varying degrees. My father has chosen not to take any medication and to endure the discomfort and pain.

Yet, what my father never loses is his desire to love—his wife, his children, his God. This love, which my father once described as "a deep impulse," becomes something he trusts.

"You're in my heart, always," my father constantly says to me during my visits. He points to his chest when he utters these words, as though he is saying something that is eternal, something that is more than his physical life.

My father has become one of my teachers, expanding my capacity to love, to feel love's sweet warmth and rough edges. Through our relationship, I have learned about forgiveness: what it means, how hard it is, and how healing it is.

My father's deep brown eyes are full with light and love now. They are beaming across the dining-room table where we share his last few meals. I have never felt anyone

look at me in this way, with the incandescence of such radi-
ant love. He is giving it all away. I tell myself: *Don't be
afraid; take it in. If love is a waterfall, then let it fall.*

———————— // ————————

Seeking Surrender

The next time you are looking into the mirror, stop for a
moment and practice gazing into your eyes. Gazing is done
with soft eyes, and it is a spiritual practice that is tradition-
ally done in front of an icon. Relax your eyes as you are
looking, becoming more gentle and loving with yourself.
See your eyes as containing the fullness of life. See the love
that is pouring out of them. For today, practice the art of
gazing. Notice what it feels like to see in this way.

———————— // ————————

Open Borders

Three years after Mark and I began our journey to surrender to the truth that we would not have children, I find
myself working in an elementary-school library, seeing
more than three hundred students a week. It is not where
I expected to land, but here I am.

Because of budget cuts, I lost my job in the head office
of the school district working on staff-development pro-
grams, and so I decided to accept an opportunity to work
in an elementary-school library. I remember the pangs I felt
during my first few weeks here at the school, as I watched

the parents holding their children's hands and walking them onto the campus. But I know now that my life cannot be reduced to getting or not getting what I want.

Over time, I settle into my new role, reading to children, helping them select books, and assisting them with research projects. I begin to enjoy the job. I find the students to be curious, sensitive, and funny, and the school community is a network of caring and creative people.

Even though my doubts and disappointments occasionally get stirred up and whirl around me, I can stand more firmly in my own experience. I have committed myself to the path of surrender, and I am not turning back. The practice and grace of surrender are now with me, and I can stay in my story with greater trust and confidence.

One day, a five-year-old girl runs up to me in the hall and just stands there hugging me. I don't ask her what is the matter. She will tell me if there is something. She just wants to be held, no questions asked. I respond to the desire, my arms wrapped across her small back, exchanging love, comfort, and the surrender of the moment.

March 28, 2007
Dear Brother René,

Greetings and happy spring! I pray for the community of Gethsemani at this special time of year. I think of you often and keep you in my prayers. I wanted to let you know what a gift you have been in my life, and how much you have given to me. You helped me along the journey of surrender. I thank you and I thank God for this gift.

I am so inspired by this experience that I am currently writing about it, and I would like to use excerpts of the letters you sent me in the project. As I reread your letters to me, I see how they helped give me the confidence and courage to trust in my life. I would like to share your understanding about surrender, and your strength, faith, and confidence in God's great love for us all.

I am enclosing a letter of permission for your consideration. I will wait to hear from you, and pray over this in the meantime.

Thank you,
Colette

April 4, 2007
Dear Colette,
Peace. Joy. Love.

Here is your letter, signed and mailed on April 4. I wish you well on your project, which is a perfect expression of surrender to God and reaching out to be an instrument of peace to others.

You place yourself in God's hands to use you as He will for His glory and the benefit of others.

Greetings to Mark.
In his Love,
Brother René

On the Voyage

I stand at the doorway of my father's bedroom, looking at him in the hospital bed that has been set up in their house through hospice care. He is wearing a white, V-neck, cotton T-shirt, which I have seen him in so many times in the hot southern California weather.

Now he is lying flat on his back, his body still and his breathing shallow; he is completely self-contained, in his voyage of surrender. I feel the urge to walk into the room, to stand near his bed and hold his hand or stroke his forehead, but something inside tells me to wait. He is traveling, and he is not to be disturbed. I have to give him the space he needs to complete the journey.

I stand at the threshold of the doorway, saying good-bye, expressing gratitude for the friendship we shared, thankful for the forgiveness that passed between us. Over the years, my father has expressed such deep sorrow for being inattentive and neglectful to me and my sisters during our childhood. Now, I place him in my heart, on the wings of God, and pray for his passage. There is a calling to surrender to the unfathomable depth of this experience.

No one is in the house but the two of us. My mother and my sister have gone out for a short walk. I do not enter his room, but I look at him, so still, in a deep sleep, enveloped in the diffused daylight that is coming through the closed blinds. It's as though I am speaking what I cannot say in words. It's a parting dance. It's a dance for the dead and for the living. I am to remain on the other side of the door. He is to go. *Goodbye; I love you; goodbye*, I hear my heart saying.

Hours later, as I stand by his bed with the evening nurse, my father exhales his last breath, shallow, thin, and final. Within seconds, his cheeks become hollow, and he no longer looks like my father.

My father has passed through the gate, returning to creation, embraced by God, and no longer separate.

The nurse calls my mother and sister into the room. My mother stands between us, holding our hands, squeezing mine so tightly I feel as if I'm holding her up. We are silently weeping, and like me, my mother doesn't want to look that closely at the shell of my father's body. I walk her over to the kitchen table and sit her down, placing her gray cashmere sweater around her shoulders. My sister and the nurse are taking care of the necessary paperwork, while I sit next to my mother still holding her hand. Neither of us wants to let go

"I love you," she says. "I thank God you are here with me."

------------------//------------------

Seeking Surrender

Hold the sacred cup of life with love. The next time you sit quietly for a few moments, try praying with the symbol of a cup. First, look around your house and find a cup to become your sacred vessel. Choose one that feels right for you. Now, in a contemplative way, hold your cup and reflect on what it might be containing for you at this sacred time—perhaps tears, loss, or joy. Do you sense a fullness or an emptiness as you gaze at it? Listen to what is stirring in your heart, and ask for the grace to see how the Divine is present in whatever your cup is holding. Is there a prayer that comes to you?

———————— // ————————

Courage

During my summer vacation, I decide to go on a retreat to rest and nurture my interior life. I attend a five-day contemplative retreat in California, facilitated by Jonathan Montaldo, the editor of many of Thomas Merton's journals.

The August weather is warm, and the retreat center is in the height of the summer season, with humming birds flitting around the courtyard fountain and the sweet smell of jasmine lingering in the garden. I look forward to bringing my breakfast and lunch tray outside and listening to the trickling water while eating in silence.

In our first session, Jonathan talks about the tradition of spiritual seekers going into the desert in fourth-century Egypt to ask one of the elders for a "word" for their salvation. The elders were known as the Desert Mothers and Fathers, and their word was intended to give guidance and spiritual insight. He invites us to listen, deep in the pockets of our hearts, to the word waiting for us, the word that will give us the guidance we now need.

On the second morning of the retreat, I am splashing cold water on my face to wake up, when the words *have courage* just come to me. I stop and look into my own brown eyes reflected in the mirror. *Have courage*, I hear myself saying.

Now, after sharing in my father's death process, not having my own children, living without my sister, being a support to my husband through his work transition, and adjusting to the changing cycles of my sleep, these words feels significant and wise. I welcome it.

Have courage, I hear myself say again. It takes courage to live a surrendered life: to face the day tired, yet find a restful attitude; to live with layers of loss but still carry hope; to meet the demands of work, with more ease; and to care for those I love as they grow older, with gentleness.

Courage is a quiet, interior action of the heart. Courage is also acceptance of the conditions and circumstances of life. It is expressed in the daily choices we make, as we hold our lives with trust. Every journey takes courage, and every experience can be a gateway to surrendering with courage, inviting us to weave our lives into the divine fabric of life.

From the quiet halls of the Gethsemani monastery, I have received more than forty letters from Brother René, always encouraging me to have the courage to walk into the center of my life—and open myself to grace.

Seeking Surrender

Ask yourself: *What is calling for my courage right now?* Reflect on your present journey of the heart, the body, and the soul.

Courage comes from encouragement. Give it to yourself. Meet yourself in your life as it is right now—not waiting for something to change or be different. Listen for the guiding word that is waiting for you. It might come to you when you're washing your face! Be open. Pay attention. Discover the word that your heart, in this moment, needs the most.

Chapter 4

Remembrance and Reflection

Several years pass, during which Brother René and I stop our regular correspondence, my father dies, and a beloved teacher faces health issues due to age. I sense Brother René, himself, has become increasingly frail. It is now 2009, seven years since I made my first visit to Gethsemani. I am acutely aware of the seasons of life, and I feel a strong desire to see him again.

That fall, I decide to head back and make a visit. I want to honor a place and the friendship that have led me on my path of surrender.

On the morning of my departure, my alarm fails to go off. When I open my eyes, the clock reads 5:25 a.m., and my flight is scheduled to leave at 6:50 a.m. I dash out of bed, quickly dress, put my packed bags in the car, and have my husband drive me to the airport. I rush to my gate and—to my amazement—make my flight. If this is a sign I am meant to go, it is loud and clear.

Once I arrive in Kentucky, I feel instantly comfortable on the grounds of the monastery, in the silence and uncluttered spaces. I am staying at the retreat house this time, in the same complex as the church and dining room, near the monks' quarters. My private room contains a single bed, a small wooden desk, an alcove for a closet, and a print of an early icon of Mary on the wall. I feel like a pilgrim, being offered shelter and a refuge from the demands of my busy life. I send Brother René a note that I have arrived.

As the bells announce the evening prayer, I enter the church and take a seat in the section reserved for guests. Time folds into itself as the past seven years seem to merge with the present moment. I sit still, absorbing what has been in my memory for so long: the birch-wood pews, the white plaster walls, the gray stone floor, and the unembellished altar. I savor the silence and the permission to be quiet.

The monks enter, and I spot Brother René in his white prayer robe, walking intently with a wooden cane. He is smaller in stature than I remember, but just as jovial and kind looking. He is now an old man.

Tears well up in my eyes, as I am overcome with affection for him and for Gethsemani. Stirring inside of me is the deep recognition that my relationship with him has profoundly influenced the path I am on. I have come to believe that God brings people together in mysterious and unpredictable ways and speaks to us through these unions. Perhaps they are the holiest and most sacred aspects of our lives.

The prayer period begins, and I comfortably join in, chanting the psalms softly along with the other guests. The steady harmony of the monks lands in my ears like a homecoming. My heart sinks into the pauses and silence. I know I belong here. I watch Brother René raise his frail frame up and down from his seat with the help of his cane, as he follows the movement of the prayers, without skipping a beat. I can see he continues to be passionate and dedicated to his life as a monk, which fills my heart with joy at being here.

Afterward, I wait in the church for Brother René. I don't know what to expect, but I have chosen to dismiss any doubts and open my heart to the experience.

When he finally appears, I stand up as he makes his way toward me.

"Colette," he says, pointing to me.

"Yes," I answer.

"I don't really recognize you," he says.

"It's my salt-and-pepper hair color," I say, smiling.

"Well, I hardly have any hair left," he says, laughing as he touches his nearly bald head. We pause and look at each other with ease and tenderness, awakening our memories. We make a plan to meet the next day at the guesthouse in the late morning.

Over the week, I meet with Brother René every day, either in the morning or late afternoon, in an intimate chapel right next to the church. Quickly, we fall into an easy rapport. Some days, we meet only briefly, if he has a doctor's appointment or phone calls to make, while other days we meet for longer, talking together about books, God, the spiritual life, our daily lives, family, or life at the monastery. We are comfortable with each other. I feel a sense of familiarity and a bond that our letters have given us.

I share with him my experience with my father dying and about my periods of insomnia, my library job, and the joy in my marriage. I confide in him my longing to surrender even more, to trust my life more deeply, and to release the weight I still carry over not being more accomplished. Once again, he encourages me to trust and have confidence that God is in everything with me and to live my life from that profound union.

He tells me about his second bout of skin cancer, though he doesn't let on how serious it is, and about the worn-out cartilage in his knee, which is why he needs a cane. He isn't complaining, and he expresses during one of our conversations that he is happy. I can tell by the radiance in his eyes that he is. He shares with me his enthusiasm for a book he is reading, *My Other Self* by Clarence Enzler, in which Christ speaks directly to the reader in a dialogue format about love, service, prayer, and other topics. He shows me the book as though he is showing me part of his soul. He reads me selected excerpts, some on death, and I see the way he is yielding to the next stage of his life, with acceptance of his life's journey.

One morning, he gives me a one-inch-thick black binder, filled with typed pages of his writing. "I hope you can read some of this while you are here," he says. "They

are the poems and dialogues I have written over the years."
I take the binder with me and place it on the desk in my
room. During the week, it isn't only our exchange of words
but also our praying together that affects and touches me.
His devotion inspires and steadies me. I participate in
the daily seven prayer periods, giving myself over to the
constant sound of the church bells to direct my actions. I
always sit within close proximity to the monks, and at the
end of each prayer period, Brother René and I exchange a
glance and gentle smile as he exits the church. In the evening, I sit next to him on a wooden pew in the small chapel
as he leads the Rosary, and I use one of the black-beaded
rosaries he has made and given to me.

One rainy afternoon, I nestle into the reading chair in
the corner of my retreat room, and as the persistent rain-
drops tap against the glass window, I read through the
binder Brother René has given me. His writing is funny,
personal, hopeful, and full of the desire to surrender.
He writes about his spiritual experiences, his intimate
moments in contemplation, and his reflections on life as
a monk.

"I's to See"
by Brother René

For several years now
I have had a large wooden crucifix
in my room.
But the corpus did not have arms.
Then one day I asked Jesus,

"What happened to your arms?"
I wore them out, He replied.

"Oh my! How did you wear them out?"
By hugging the people I love,
He answered me.

And then He added,
Can I use yours?
"Of course, of course, yes, yes, please do!
Here they are! Use them as you will!"
I blurted out.

No, keep them where they are:
Leave them in place.
When I need them,
as I do every day,
I will let you know.

And if people I send
resist or turn away,
and perhaps leave you wounded besides,
then remember
you too at times have felt like sandpaper.
"I'm sorry, Lord!"

Never mind, just go ahead
and wear 'em out for me.

And please remember
and acknowledge

how it is I in them
who is embracing you.

All are my servants
and I use them
as much as they allow me to.

"But, Lord, I still slip!"

Indeed you do—still, have I ever let you down?
"Oh, no, Lord! Never and I thank you."

Love will always win in the end,
just as I did with you.

Come—let's dance!

Surrender is a living force at the monastery. I notice it in the faithfulness of the monks, as they arrive in the church for the seven prayer periods, hour after hour, day and night, always making a broad Sign of the Cross across their chests as they enter and bow toward the altar. I hear it in the psalms we chant, "In you, Lord, I place all my trust" and I see it in the burnt-red sunsets filling the wide open sky. I sense it in the silence of the guests as they close their eyes and sink deep inside themselves during prayer. I feel it in my compliant body, with the 3:00 a.m. bells calling me to Vigils.

Here, again, on the grounds of the monastery, in the midst of the rain and the dark early mornings, I find my heart stirring and hear the call. I finally understand. Living is surrendering. I am being called to stay faithful to the journey and to keep opening to a greater will than just my own—that of creation, of the Divine, and of the pulsing spirit of life bursting forth in every cell, in every seed, in every tree, in every smile, in every breath. Once more, the Trappist monks, Brother René, and the rolling hills of Kentucky open my interior gate to the resounding call of surrender ringing in each strike of the bells in the abbey's church tower.

On my last morning, Brother René and I sit in the chapel. We talk about the beauty of the early-morning Vigils, and he comments, "You looked so peaceful when I looked over at you." We spend time reviewing his writing, and he is grateful for my feedback and input. He has me mark my comments and edits on the pages. His niece is planning to compile his writing into a chapbook. Once again, we have found a way to give each other what we are seeking.

At the end of our conversation, I ask Brother René, "What is the heart of the spiritual life?" His answer is short and simple. "It is love," he says. "So always live in love."

We hug goodbye. And as I sit in the taxi to the airport and land back in San Francisco with my husband waiting, these are the words I remember.

On April 10, 2011, Brother René returned to the source of love. I am infinitely grateful for the friendship we shared.

Chapter 5

Learning to Walk the Path of Surrender

While walking along the path of surrender, I experienced a constant tension between surrender and resistance. Surrender pulled in the direction of ease and acceptance, while resistance pushed back with doubt and anger. I interacted with them both, until I no longer related to them as oppositional. I came to understand they moved together across the landscape of my days, like wind.

Over time, I began to see that whenever I brushed up against my own resistance, I would find an unexpected invitation to surrender; and each time I turned and opened toward surrender, I would meet some degree of resistance. I became more attuned to the qualities of surrender and of resistance—in the thoughts they each generated, in the sensations they created in my body, and in the feelings they aroused in my heart. In this dynamic interplay, I realized I could encourage, pray for, and choose to let the path of surrender take the lead. Eventually, I found a new way to be in my life, one that did not parse out the last decade into piles labeled good or bad, success or failure, but that instead gave me more trust and faith in my path.

As surrender became my new foundation, I was able to accept and embrace my life, and dwell more in the mystery of it. I became a spiritual director and found myself comforting people in times of grief. I allowed myself to laugh more generously with the children I worked with in the library. My husband and I become a family, the two of us, caring for our home, sharing meals, and celebrating holidays—sometimes with friends or extended family, always with a satisfying feeling of completeness. And I, with an inner strength that I had not known before, followed the inspiration to write this book about my surrender journey and the profound importance of the spiritual friendship I shared with Brother René.

It was not willpower that created this shift. I could only do so much on my own. Yet, I realized that I didn't need to rely solely on myself. I wasn't dangling from a thin thread, or about to fall into the void. I was actually being held, carried, and embraced by the power of love, the fullness of creation, and the presence and action of the Divine living in me and all around me. I thank Brother René for the gift of this message.

Still, this did not mean that my will ceased, for there are many types of will, not just the one of determination. In the act of surrender, the spiritual will, the compassionate will, and the merciful will come forward with fortitude and resilience.

I now believe that when we arrive at the threshold of surrender, we are usually at our lowest point. We are exhausted and vulnerable from loss, disappointment, and sadness. We are grief stricken and do not want to be where we have landed. For a long time, we have been holding on, waiting for things to turn, but nothing has changed.

In this darkness, in this collapse, the light of surrender enters, penetrating what is dense and covering us, until it reaches the innermost chamber of our heart. There it offers us the gift of healing. It is a sacred juncture, beyond our grasp, asking us to trust more than our limited capacity can understand.

Looking back, I recognize five major steps in my journey of surrender. I found that my experience was more circular than linear. The stages and movements repeat and overlap. I'd like to share them with you.

Step 1: Acknowledge

By acknowledging what we cannot change or control, we begin to pave the way for surrender to enter our lives. We must not be afraid of our grief and our suffering. Eventually, I sat in the immense depth of mine, not trying to get over anything, but allowing myself to be with what I was feeling and experiencing.

Although piercing and painful, the release and opening that happens through honest reflection can create a receptive ground for surrender to take root and grow. By holding our pain in a truthful and gentle way, we bring compassion to ourselves and our circumstances. This happens by staying still and not running away from what we are feeling.

In this process, we must have confidence that something new will be created from our brokenness. Through patience and the willingness to heal, we will integrate our sadness and grief, holding our story with integrity and comfort. As my mother wisely taught me through her journey recovering from alcoholism, people don't get over things, but over time, they learn to carry the experiences of their lives with more understanding, forgiveness, and compassion. As we allow healing to permeate our pain, we in turn can become a healing force in the world for others.

Try practicing acknowledgment using the following steps:

1. Find a comfortable and safe place to be still and quiet with yourself.
2. Remember that you are not alone and that you are connected to all that is sacred to you. Call out to your God for assistance.
3. Feel your feelings. Let them be strong. Cry if you need to, or let yourself shout with anger. It is important to pay close attention to the quality of your feelings because at some point they will peak and then begin to subside.

4. Let go. Let the feelings move through you. By not holding on, you are trusting that you are passing through a
   gate to more freedom and peace.
5. Be gentle and compassionate with yourself. You might
   want to take a bath or sit quietly and let your body relax
   after experiencing such strong emotions.

Repeat this process as many times as you need. After
each time, close by saying, "I trust I am healing."

Step 2: Find Support and Solitude

I found support along the way from Brother René, my husband, my spiritual director, friends, and different creative
and spiritual groups of people, as well as from my elderly
father and mother, who, from their own pain, were willing
to sit with me in mine and not try to force me to get over
what I was feeling and experiencing.

We are not alone in our journey. We all experience
loss, grief, loneliness, disappointment, and we all have a
desire for healing. Therefore, it is important to find others to connect with on our journey, either through affinity
groups, a spiritual community, family and friends, or any
healing or supportive network.

Finding support requires the willingness to reach out
to others, as well as the recognition of who is reaching out
to us when we open ourselves to support. By sharing our
circumstances and stories with each other, we receive the
compassion and encouragement we need to hear the call
of surrender in our lives and to move forward.

Yet, we must also remember that the journey of surrender is a deeply personal one. At times we need solitude. We need to be alone in order to settle into the story of our lives. As we sink into a more interior level, we find comfort, compassion, and strength from our relationship with the Divine, our relationship with our deepest self, and from what we hold most sacred.

Surrender is an intimate journey, and we must honor the time we need. It's a period of discernment and reflection, which can bring us closer to ourselves and to God, who is, as I learned from Brother René, our constant companion.

In deciding on your need for support, the following suggestions can serve as a guide:

1. Find people and groups you can trust with what you are going through. Ask for recommendations, and do research. Identify specific people or groups; make a list; and commit to making at least one call a week until you connect with what's right for you.
2. Find support, comfort, and compassion from your spiritual path. Go on a retreat, join a meditation group, or reach out to others in your current spiritual community.
3. Honor the time you may need alone, and give it to yourself.

Step 3: Express and Release

My infertility, my sister's cancer, my father's illness, my husband's business loss, and even my sleeplessness felt like an intense, never-ending confrontation with the human condition. A pressure had built up in me from the years of exerting so much effort to effect what ultimately I could not control.

I needed to release all I had stored up in myself. I cried. I wrote. I prayed. I painted. I swam. I walked for hours. I cleaned out my closets. And I cared for others. All of these turned out to be part of my healing process.

Writing became the primary way for me to express myself—to rant, to rave, to mourn, to question, to cry out to God. I scribbled and scrawled my way through tunnels of feelings, questions, doubts, and rage. The writing became a form of discovering the surrender that was seeking to be heard. As I wrote in notebooks, journals, and in my letters to Brother René, I began to hear the call to surrender, to trust God, and to let go.

There are many forms of expression available to us. We can sing, dance, work in our garden, take long walks, paint the rooms in our house, keep a journal, or even start a creative project. The method is not as important as the critical need to find a way to express and release all the energy moving around inside us, to listen to what is stirring, and not to push our thoughts and feelings away.

This is a time to release what has built up inside of us and not hold on to it. By engaging in a form of creative expression, we are participating in our own healing process. The more we can let go of what has accumulated inside of us, the more we clear the way for surrender.

Remember what is said in the Gospel of Thomas: "If you bring forth what is within you, what you bring forth will save you. If you do not bring forth what is within you, what you do not bring forth will destroy you."[8]

Here are some ways to engage in creative expression as a tool for releasing and letting go:

1. Find expression for your voice by writing in a journal or notebook using this simple writing prompt: "Today, I would like to say . . ." Express all your feelings, and don't hold back. After each writing period, write at the bottom of the page: "I have faith that expressing myself is healing." Try this practice daily for a month, and discover how healing it can be.

2. Find expression for your voice by drawing your feelings. Draw your anger, sadness, compassion, self-love, and everything and anything that will support you in releasing all you are feeling over a certain situation that you would like to surrender. It's fine if your drawings are scribbles, lines, and big forms of color. After each drawing period, write at the bottom of the page: "I have faith that expressing myself is healing." Try this practice daily for a month, and discover how healing it can be.

3. Find expression for your voice by engaging in movement, through an expressive dance class or by turning up the music and dancing in your living room.

Step 4: Seek Spiritual Nourishment

I gave myself freedom to seek spiritual nourishment in many ways. I engaged in different prayer forms by participating in the ritual of the Mass, sitting in meditation, and reading books by spiritual teachers and mystics. I also joined in Taizé, a form of chanting and repeating prayers set to music. Prayer gave me sustenance along the way, nurtured my connection to the Divine, and became my anchor in the moving waters of my experience.

Through openness and discernment, I discovered prayers and practices that gave me comfort, strength, and healing. I found the work of the contemporary Vietnamese Buddhist monk Thich Nhat Hanh to offer me a way to bring compassion to my pain and ease the heaviness that had settled in my heart. On a retreat with Thich Nhat Hanh, I learned to embrace my pain as tenderly as a mother would hold her baby, while mindfully repeating the phrase: *Breathing in, I am holding my pain. Breathing out, I am with my pain.*

In this practice, there exists no judgment or pressure to get over what we are feeling. It is simply a way of bringing our love and attention to what is happening in the present moment. It is a practice of allowing release to happen at a deep cellular level by meeting our suffering with love and compassion.

Along the way, I also engaged in Metta meditation, a Buddhist practice in which one recites words and phrases to evoke love. If I would see a woman with a child and begin to feel upset, I would repeat: *May I be happy and at peace; may you be happy and at peace; may we be happy and at peace.* Through the power of this compassionate action, I cultivated a loving feeling toward myself and others and broke through layers of loss, grief, and habits of comparison.

Another prayer I frequently recited and found deeply consoling was one by Saint Ignatius of Loyola, from the sixteenth century. It is a prayer of total surrender:

> Take, Lord, and receive all my liberty, my memory, my understanding, and my entire will. All that I have and call my own. You have given all to me. To you, Lord, I return it. Everything is yours: do with it what you will. Give me only your love and grace; that is enough for me.

Being in nature also emerged as a way of prayer for me. As I would take a long walk by the ocean, I found myself absorbing all that was being offered. I watched the pelicans gliding low across the water with the ocean mist on my cheeks. The cool blue sky soared above me; I was able to embrace creation and feel a part of it with delightful awe.

We must each find *our* way of praying—and trust and practice it. The spiritual life is boundless, creative, intimate, and waiting for us to make it our own.

I noticed that the more I stopped trying to define God or name every bird I saw flying by, the vastness opened up. Prayer became a way for me to be in deeper relationship with my life, with creation, and with what was sacred all around me. Prayer became the heart of my journey of surrender.

Here are some suggestions to help you connect to the power of prayer:

1. Name and claim all the ways you pray and hold what is most sacred—such as by being in nature, through quiet contemplation, by singing or crying, or by painting, swimming, or reading sacred texts. Make a commitment to pray every day in some form. It is the intention to connect to the sacred that is the most important.
2. Find places or people that encourage your spiritual joy and growth, and make a connection with them. Is it a yoga studio, a church, or a gardening group? Make a list, and discover what is right for you.
3. Try a new method or way of prayer that you are curious about and would like to explore. Find a labyrinth near you, practice the daily examen, keep a spiritual journal, or learn to meditate. Find what inspires you.

Step 5: Notice Opportunities to Surrender in Daily Life

Our everyday encounters create the platform for surrender. Throughout the day, we can bring the qualities of surrender into the way we respond: with trust, acceptance, compassion, and release. It is our relationship to what is happening that forms the cornerstone of our experiences.

The call to surrender is present in all our lives. I see it in my mother-in-law, who is still working in her seventies although she'd prefer to retire, and in one of my sisters, who is struggling to accept the choices of her adult children. I notice it in my friend, who is surrendering to her creativity and making big, bold paintings after years of timid drawing. I find it in my brother, who had to change careers later in his life. And I witness it in those who are aging, such as my elderly mother, who now uses a walker to get around.

Surrender happens in our daily lives, the ones we are actually living. It is not a spiritual ideal for saints and holy people but, rather, a living and dynamic force that moves in and through us. Surrender is an invitation to find contentment and peace, today and tomorrow, to open ourselves to trust life beyond the limitations that our fears, our expectations, and our disappointments impose on it.

Along the way, rage will return, grief will overtake us, loss will come knocking at our door, and doubt will be a constant visitor. But if we seek and build surrender as our foundation, it will hold us in those darker moments, allowing grace to move us forward along our path.

Every day, we are being called to surrender—in love, in faith, in work, in relationships, in our hearts, in our bodies, and in every breath we take. Letting go, yielding to what is, and releasing what we are clinging to takes great courage. But when we do, we invite acceptance, trust, and divine love into the center of our lives, and in that embrace, in that sacred place where our joys and sorrows meet and heaven and earth touch, we are drawn, despite all our resistance, toward the sweetness of surrender.

Notes

1. Thomas Merton, *Thoughts in Solitude* (New York: Farrar, Shraus, Giroux, 1986), 79.

2. Thomas Merton, *A Search for Solitude: The Journals of Thomas Merton*, vol. 3 (San Francisco: Harper Collins, 1996), 211.

3. Thomas Merton, *The Intimate Thomas Merton: His Life from His Journals* (New York: Harper Collins), 113.

4. Ibid., 130.

5. John XXIII, *Journal of a Soul: The Autobiography of Pope John XXIII* (New York: Image Books, 1999), 276.

6. Ibid.

7. Ibid.

8. Elaine Pagels, *Beyond Belief: The Secret Gospel of Thomas* (New York: Vintage Books, 2004), XV.

Collette Lafia is a San Francisco-based blogger, spiritual director, workshop and retreat facilitator, and part-time school librarian. She is an adjunct faculty member at Mercy Center Burlingame, where she also earned two certificates in spiritual direction. Lafia has a bachelor's degree in creative writing and English from San Francisco State University and a master's of library information science from San Jose State University. She is the author of *Comfort and Joy: Simple Ways to Care for Ourselves and Others.*

AVE MARIA PRESS

Founded in 1865, Ave Maria Press,
a ministry of the Congregation of
Holy Cross, is a Catholic publishing
company that serves the spiritual and
formative needs of the Church and its
schools, institutions, and ministers;
Christian individuals and families; and
others seeking spiritual nourishment.

———⊷⊷———

For a complete listing of titles from

Ave Maria Press

Sorin Books

Forest of Peace

Christian Classics

visit www.avemariapress.com

AVE MARIA PRESS
Notre Dame, IN
A Ministry of the United States Province of Holy Cross